INTO

RELIGIOUS EDUCATION

Christianity:
Origins and
Contemporary Expressions

Thomas Norris
& Brendan Leahy

Series Editors
Eoin G. Cassidy and Patrick M. Devitt

VERITAS

First published 2004 by
Veritas Publications
7/8 Lower Abbey Street
Dublin 1
Ireland
Email publications@veritas.ie
Website www.veritas.ie

ISBN 1 85390 796 0

10 9 8 7 6 5 4 3 2 1

Copyright © Thomas Norris and Brendan Leahy, 2004

The material in this publication is protected by copyright law. Except as may be permitted by law, no part of the material may be reproduced (including by storage in a retrieval system) or transmitted in any form or by any means, adapted, rented or lent without the written permission of the copyright owners. Applications for permissions should be addressed to the publisher.

A catalogue record for this book is available from the British Library.

Cover design by Bill Bolger
Printed in the Republic of Ireland by Betaprint Ltd, Dublin

Veritas books are printed on paper made from the wood pulp of managed forests. For every tree felled, at least one tree is planted, thereby renewing natural resources.

Contents

Series Introduction 5

Preface 15

A Selection of Dates in the History of Christianity 17

1. The Return to Origins 21

2. The Vision of Jesus in Context 59

3. The Message in Conflict 89

4. The Formation of Christian Community 121

5. The Christian Message Today 149

Series Introduction

September 2003 saw the introduction of the Leaving Certificate Religious Education Syllabus by the Department of Education and Science. For those concerned to promote a religious sensibility in young Irish adults it is hard to exaggerate the importance of this event. It both represents a formal recognition by society of the value of religious education in the academic lives of second-level students, and it also reflects the importance which Irish society attaches to promoting the personal growth of students, including their spiritual and moral development. Religious education offers young people the opportunity to understand and interpret their experience in the light of a religious world-view. Furthermore, in and through an engagement with the RE Syllabus at Leaving Certificate level, students will learn a language that will enable them both to articulate their own faith experience and to dialogue with those of different faiths or non-theistic stances.

The Department of Education Syllabus is to be welcomed in that it gives recognition to the role that religious education plays in the human development of the young person. It is not an exaggeration to say that religious education is the capstone of the school's educational response to the young person's search for meaning and values. In this context, it encourages students to reflect upon their awareness of themselves as unique individuals with roots in a community network of family, friends and parish. Furthermore, it allows students to acknowledge and reflect upon their relationship to a God who cares for them and for the world in which we live. Finally, it gives students access to the universal nature of the quest for truth, beauty and goodness. Most of these themes are addressed sympathetically in the section entitled *The Search for Meaning and Values*. In particular, this section is to be welcomed because it offers the possibility for students to grapple with theistic and non-theistic world-views in a context that is hospitable to religious belief.

A critical dimension of the young person's educational journey is the growth in understanding of their own culture and the manner in which culture shapes their outlook on the world. The Religious Education Syllabus not only addresses the manner in which religion (and in particular Christianity) has shaped Irish culture over many centuries, but it also provides an extremely valuable platform from which to critique aspects of the relationship between faith and culture in the contemporary world. The section entitled *Religion: The Irish Experience* addresses the former concern by showing pupils the manner in which the Christian religion has contributed to the belief patterns and values of Irish society. It also alerts them to the depths of religious belief that predate by many centuries, even millennia, the arrival of Christianity in Ireland; and it also connects them to the cultural richness that links Ireland to the European continent. In this context, the devotional revolution that took place in Ireland (including the extraordinary growth in religious orders from 1850-1930) is a topic that could be expanded. The missionary outreach of the Catholic Church in Ireland in the last hundred years is worthy of special mention. Finally, students studying this section should be encouraged to acknowledge the ambiguities that have attended the presence of religion in Ireland over the centuries; to see on the one hand the image of an island of saints and scholars, and on the other hand to note how 'lilies that fester smell far worse than weeds'. In examining the manner in which faith and culture interact, the sections entitled *Religion and Science* and *Religion and Gender* make a valuable contribution to the Syllabus. These sections address topical issues that were controversial in the past and continue to be problematical even today. In treating of these two topics it is obviously important to avoid stereotypes – the acceptance of unexamined assumptions that mask or over-simply the truth to such an extent as to do a disservice to the seriousness of the issues involved. Likewise, the section on *World Religions* should be taught in a manner that is sensitive to the dangers of cultural and religious stereotypes. This section not only gives students a valuable introduction to the main religions in the world, but it also provides a cultural context for an awareness of the fact that the phenomenon of religion and the experience of religious belief is something that shapes people's understanding of themselves and their lifestyles across all cultural boundaries. Furthermore, it should never be forgotten that if, as Christians believe, God's Spirit is present in and through these religions, there is a need to study these religions precisely in order to discover aspects of God's presence in the world that has the capability to continually surprise.

In the Irish cultural context, Catholicism shapes the religious sensibilities and practices of the majority of young people. The Syllabus offers a generous acknowledgement of the importance of Christianity in the Irish context by providing two sections that focus on core aspects of the Christian faith. These are: *Christianity: Origins and Contemporary Expressions* and *The Bible: Literature and Sacred text*. In this context, the Syllabus section on the Bible is to be welcomed. However, greater attention could be given to the role and significance of the Prophets in the Old Testament and to Paul in the New Testament. Furthermore, in studying the Bible it should never be forgotten that the primary reality is not the 'book' but rather the person of Christ and the community tradition grappling with this reality that is revealed in and through the Bible.

What is often in danger of being forgotten in an academic context is the importance of the fostering of attitudes and practices that promote personal growth. Religious education cannot be focused only on knowledge and understanding, because religion is primarily a way of celebrating life and, in particular, the spiritual dimension of life in and through the practices of worship, ritual and prayer. The Syllabus' recognition of this critical dimension of religious education through the section entitled *Worship, Ritual and Prayer* is to be welcomed. In addressing this section of the Syllabus it would be important to alert students to the great variety of spiritualities, prayer forms, mysticisms, rituals and styles of music that are to be found within the Christian tradition in order that students may have the possibility of exploring the richness of the spiritual dimension of their own tradition.

A key remit of the educational process is the fostering of moral maturity through a syllabus that allows students to engage in moral education. Not only is religious education particularly suited to facilitating this educational imperative, but the ethical character of human life is a core feature of all religions. The importance of this dimension of religious education is recognised in the provision of two sections entitled *Moral Decision Making* and *Issues of Justice and Peace*. There is nothing optional about the challenge to promote justice and peace. However, it is a topic that can all too easily be ideologically driven. Therefore, there is a special responsibility on those teaching this section to ensure that the instances of injustice cited, and the causes of injustice proposed, are grounded in solid research.

The challenges to Catholic religion teachers
Though religious education has been an integral part of Irish second-level schools long before the foundation of the state, it

has not until now been possible to assess this work under the State examination system. The reason for this anomaly is the Intermediate Education Act (1878) which allowed for the teaching but forbade the State examination of religious education. The removal of this legal constraint on State examination of RE has provided the impetus for the introduction of the Junior Certificate Syllabus in September 2000 and the introduction of the Leaving Certificate Syllabus in September 2003. These changes are to be welcomed but they provide a number of major challenges to Catholic religion teachers that should not be minimised.

In the *first* place, Catholic religion teachers have to attend to the danger that the new Syllabus will lead to a weakening of a commitment to catechesis in second level schools. The catechetical project of faith formation is built around six key pillars: knowledge of the faith; liturgical/sacramental education; moral formation; learning to pray; education for community life, including a fostering of the ecumenical character of Christian community, and finally, missionary initiative and inter-religious dialogue. Clearly, the RE Leaving Certificate Syllabus does give attention to many of the above themes, including the key catechetical concerns of attitude or value formation and the development of commitments. However, the emphasis in the Syllabus is undoubtedly upon the acquiring of knowledge, understanding and knowledge-based skills, all of which undoubtedly place it under the rubric of religious education rather than catechesis. The religion teacher ought to value the distinctive approaches to religion reflected in both catechesis and religious education. Both are important because both contribute in distinctive ways to the religious development of the young person. Catechesis aims at maturity of faith whereas religious education aims at knowledge and understanding of the faith.

From the point of view of the religion teacher, the teaching can have a different tone at different times. On one occasion, it might have a 'showing how' or catechetical tone, one that assumes a shared faith experience and encourages active participation. At another time it can have an educational or 'explaining' tone that invites pupils to stand back from religion to a certain extent, so that they can gain a more objective understanding of what is being taught. The Religious Education Syllabus should be taught in a manner that keeps both of these approaches in balance. In a similar vein, the presence of RE on the Leaving Certificate curriculum should not distract teachers from acknowledging that the religious development of young people happens in many contexts, which are distinct, though complementary. It can take place at home, in the parish, with friends as well as in school. Furthermore, even in the school it can take place at a whole series of levels including liturgy, prayer and projects that encourage an awareness of the need to care for those in most need.

In the *second* place, teachers have to attend to the scope and range of the aims of the Syllabus, one that seeks both to introduce students to a broad range of religious traditions and to the non-religious interpretation of life as well as providing students with the opportunity to develop an informed and critical understanding of the Christian tradition. In this context, teachers have to balance the need to promote tolerance for and mutual understanding of those of other or no religious traditions, alongside the need to give explicit attention to the Christian faith claims that Jesus is the Son of God and that he died to save us and to unite us with God and one another. Similarly, in teaching Christianity, teachers need to give attention to the role and significance of the Church from a Catholic perspective. It should never be forgotten that the idea of the Church as 'people of God', 'body of Christ' and 'temple of the Holy Spirit' is one that is at the heart of Catholic self-understanding.

In a similar vein, the Syllabus encourages students to engage critically with a wide variety of ethical codes with a view to the development of a moral maturity. Teachers will have to balance this approach with the way in which morality is viewed within the Christian tradition under the heading of discipleship – Jesus invites people to follow *him* rather than an ethical code or vision. Furthermore, from a Christian perspective, morality is never simply or even primarily concerned with a listing of moral prohibitions, rather it situates the ethical dimension of human nature within the context of a belief in a forgiving God. Finally, it should not be forgotten that it does not make sense to teach morality in too abstract a manner. Morality is something preeminently practical and at all times needs to be brought down to the level of real people – those who struggle with the demands of conscience in their lives. From a Catholic perspective, one has in the lives of the saints a multitude of examples of the manner in which people have attempted to follow the call to discipleship that is Christian morality.

Finally, nobody concerned with the seriousness of the challenge facing schools to promote moral maturity could be unaware of the importance of the contemporary challenge posed to the promotion of societal and religious values by the rise of a relativist and/or subjectivist ethos. In this context, the teaching of the broad variety of moral codes will have to be done in a manner that draws students' attention to the importance of acknowledging the objective nature of morality as opposed to accepting uncritically either a relativist or a subjectivist standpoint. In the light of the need to critique an exaggerated acceptance of pluralism, there is also a need to acknowledge that not all theories are equally valid, and moral decision-making is not simply a matter of applying one's own personal preference.

What is proposed in these commentaries
Given the breadth and scope of the Syllabus it is undoubtedly true that teachers will have to attend to the wide variety of sections in the Syllabus which demand a breadth of knowledge that some may find a little daunting. Even though it is not envisaged that teachers would attempt to teach all ten sections

of the Syllabus to any one group of students, nevertheless, the Syllabus will make demands upon teachers that can only be met if there are support services in place. For example, apart from the need to ensure the publishing of good quality teaching and learning resources, the schools themselves will need to ensure that appropriate resources – books, CDs, internet and videos – are provided. Finally, teachers will need to be provided with appropriate in-service training. It is to furthering this goal of providing good quality teaching and learning resources that the present series of volumes is addressed.

The eleven volumes in this series of commentaries comprise an introductory volume (already published, *Willingly To School*) that reflects upon the challenge of RE as an examination subject, along with ten other volumes that mirror the ten sections in the Syllabus. These commentaries on the Syllabus have been published to address the critical issue of the need to provide resources for the teaching of the Syllabus that are both academically rigorous and yet accessible to the educated general reader. Although primarily addressed to both specialist and general teachers of religion and third-level students studying to be religion teachers, the commentaries will be accessible to parents of Leaving Certificate pupils and, in addition, it is to be hoped that they will provide an important focus for adults in parish-based or other religious education or theology programmes. In the light of this focus, each of the volumes is structured in order to closely reflect the content of the Syllabus and its order of presentation. Furthermore, they are written in clear, easily accessible language and each includes an explanation of new theological and philosophical perspectives.

The volumes offered in this series are as follows

Patrick M. Devitt:	*Willingly to School: Religious Education as an Examination Subject*
Eoin G. Cassidy:	*The Search for Meaning and Values*
Thomas Norris and Brendan Leahy:	*Christianity: Origins and Contemporary Expressions*
Philip Barnes:	*World Religions*
Patrick Hannon:	*Moral Decision Making*
Sandra Cullen:	*Religion and Gender*
John Murray:	*Issues of Justice and Peace*
Christopher O'Donnell:	*Worship, Prayer and Ritual*
Benedict Hegarty:	*The Bible: Literature and Sacred Text*
John Walsh:	*Religion: The Irish Experience*
Fachtna McCarthy and Joseph McCann:	*Religion and Science*

Thanks are due to the generosity of our contributors who so readily agreed to write a commentary on each of the sections in the new Leaving Certificate Syllabus. Each of them brings to their commentary both academic expertise and a wealth of experience in the teaching of their particular area. In the light of this, one should not underestimate the contribution that they will make to the work of preparing teachers for this challenging project. Thanks are also due to our publishers, Veritas. Their unfailing encouragement and practical support has been of inestimable value to us and has ensured that these volumes saw the light of day. Finally, we hope that you the reader will find each of these commentaries helpful as you negotiate the paths of a new and challenging syllabus.

Eoin G. Cassidy
Patrick M. Devitt
Series Editors

Preface

This book is a commentary on section B of the new Leaving Certificate Religious Education Syllabus entitled 'Christianity: Origins and Contemporary Expressions'. We hope you find it useful.

The topic of Christianity is vast. Your reading of these pages will be enriched by consulting a variety of sources, including other contributions in this series, especially the chapters 'Christianity' in Philip Barnes' *World Religions*, 'Christianity in Ireland' in J.R. Walsh's *Religion: the Irish Experience* and Christopher O'Donnell's *Worship, Prayer and Ritual*. For Christian doctrine see *The Catechism of the Catholic Church*.

We would like to thank the series editors, Frs Patrick Devitt and Eoin Cassidy, for their encouragement and patience along the way.

Jesus Christ has been at the heart of the faith of the Irish throughout the centuries. The presence of the One often called 'Mac Mhuire', Son of Mary, was experienced everywhere, as expressed in St Patrick's Breastplate, written not later than the 700s, and which some consider to be composed by Patrick himself:

> Christ with me, Christ before me,
> Christ behind me, Christ within me,

Christ beneath me, Christ above me,
Christ on my right, Christ on my left...
Christ in the heart of everyone who thinks of me,
Christ in the mouth of everyone who speaks to me,
Christ in every eye that sees me,
Christ in every ear that hears me.
I arise today,
Through a mighty strength, the invocation of the Trinity,
Through belief in the threeness,
Through confession of the oneness
Of the Creator of Creation.

The Christian adventure continues. It is important to remember our Christian heritage. It is also vital to listen to what the Spirit is saying to the Church today (cf. Rev 2:7) because his word tells us: 'See, I am doing something new' (Is 43:18-19).

Thomas Norris and Brendan Leahy
St Patrick's Day, 2004.

A Selection of Dates in the History of Christianity

c. 28-30:	The public ministry of Jesus of Nazareth.
c. 30:	Jesus' death on the cross, the resurrection, Pentecost, the first preaching about Christ.
36:	The first persecution, dispersion and preaching of the Gospel in the countryside of Judea and Samaria (Acts 8:1-4); Paul's conversion (Acts 9).
c. 50:	Paul establishes the Church in Corinth.
60-100:	The first three Gospels are written.
64:	Great fire of Rome; Nero persecutes the Christians; the martyrdom of Peter.
112:	Letter of Pliny to the Emperor Trajan, mentioning the Christians as harmless.
c. 125-202:	Irenaeus, Bishop of Lyons. Often considered the first theologian. He also wrote on Apostolic Succession.
305:	Anthony of Egypt begins colony of hermits in the desert. It's the beginning of monasticism.
313:	Constantine's Edict of Toleration from Milan. Beginning of Christianity as the religion of the State.
325:	Council of Nicaea declaring Jesus' divinity 'one in being with the Father'.
337:	Constantine baptised on his death-bed.
346:	Death of Pachomius (Egypt), author of a famous monastic rule.
381:	First Council of Constantinople: the see of Constantinople assigned 'seniority of honour' after Rome.

395:	Augustine becomes Bishop of Hippo. He dies in 430.
410:	Sack of Rome by the Goths.
431:	Council of Ephesus affirms Mary as *Theotokos* ('Godbearer').
432:	Patrick's mission to Ireland.
451:	Council of Chalcedon states that Jesus Christ is one person 'in two natures'.
c. 586:	Columbanus leaves Ireland and travels as a missionary through Gaul and reaches Bobbio in Italy.
622:	The Hegira, year 0 of the Muslim calendar.
792:	Death of Mael Ruáin, one of the founders of the Céilí Dé current of renewal in the Irish Church.
800:	Coronation of Charlemagne as Holy Roman Emperor by Pope Leo III.
c. 800:	The Book of Kells.
1054:	Mutual excommunication pronounced in Constantinople by Papal representative, Cardinal Humbert, and Patriarch Michael Cerularius.
1075:	Condemnation of Lay Investiture by Pope Gregory.
1095:	First Crusade.
c. 1170-1221:	Dominic Guzman.
1181-1226:	Francis of Assisi.
1274:	Thomas Aquinas, Dominican theologian, dies.
1304:	Birth of Petrarch.
1309:	Papacy moved to Avignon.
1347:	Birth of St Catherine of Siena.
1378-1417:	The Great Schism.
1431:	Execution of St Joan of Arc.
1453:	Fall of Constantinople to the Turks.
1493:	Pope Alexander VI divides the new discoveries between Spain and Portugal.
1506:	Foundation of the new St Peter's Basilica.

1508:	Michelangelo paints the ceiling of the Sistine Chapel in Rome.
1517:	Luther posts the 95 theses at Wittenberg (31 October).
1521:	Luther excommunicated.
1522-2:	Ignatius of Loyola writes the *Spiritual Exercises*.
1536:	John Calvin, author of *Institutes*, arrives in Geneva.
1545-1563:	Council of Trent. Catholic Church responds to Reformation.
1555:	Peace of Augsburg. Principle of *'cuius regio eius religio'*. ('Whose region, his religion').
1572:	Year of the experience of union with God that Teresa of Avila describes as 'spiritual marriage' in her book *The Interior Castle*.
1618-48:	Thirty Years' War.
1633:	Daughters of Charity founded by Vincent de Paul and Louise de Marillac.
1801:	Birth of John Henry Newman.
1829:	Catholic Emancipation Act.
1846:	Formation of *The Evangelical Alliance* in England.
1854:	Pope Pius IX declares the immaculate conception of the Virgin Mary as an article of the Catholic faith.
1869-70:	First Vatican Council. Definition of Papal Infallibility.
1910:	Edinburgh Missionary Conference. Beginning of Modern Ecumenical Movement.
1932:	International Eucharistic Congress held in the Phoenix Park, Dublin.
1948:	Foundation of World Council of Churches in Amsterdam.
1962-65:	Second Vatican Council called by Pope John XXIII. Numerous observers both of other Christian Churches and other faith communities.

1968:	The Second General Conference of Latin American Bishops in Medellin declares an 'option for the poor'.
1970:	Pope Paul VI declares Sts Teresa of Avila and Catherine of Siena 'doctors of the Church'.
1973:	First Irish Inter-Church Meeting held in Ballymascanlon.
1978:	Election of Karol Wojtyla as Pope John Paul II.
1979:	Pope John Paul II visits Ireland.
1979:	Nobel Peace Prize awarded to Mother Teresa.
1980:	Archbishop Oscar Romero of El Salvador is assassinated.
1986:	Assisi Meeting of representatives of world religions gather together for Prayer for Peace.
1989:	Fall of the Wall of Berlin. Collapse of Communism.
1994:	Publication of the Catechism of the Catholic Church.
1997:	Thérèse of Lisieux is declared thirty-third and youngest 'Doctor of the Church' by John Paul II.
1999:	Joint Lutheran World Federation and Roman Catholic Church *Declaration on Justification*.
1999:	John Paul II declares Bridget of Sweden, Catherine of Siena and Edith Stein patrons of Europe.
2000:	Millennium Jubilee Celebrations. Among the high points: World Youth Day in August.
2002:	Second Assisi gathering of leaders and representatives for peace.
2003:	Archbishop Rowan Williams enthroned as Archbishop of Canterbury.
2003:	Mother Teresa beatified at a ceremony in St Peter's, Rome.

I

The Return to Origins

1.1 THE PATTERN OF RETURN

'Christianity' is the world religion made up of those who follow Jesus Christ as their Lord and leader, inspiration and teacher, Saviour and brother. It derives its name from the Greek word 'Christos', meaning the 'Anointed One' of God, a title given to Jesus of Nazareth who was born around 6–4 BCE and died around 30 CE.

In the *Oxford Concise Dictionary of World Religions*, we read: 'Christianity exists in a vast diversity of different styles and forms of organization, but all agree that the figure of Jesus is the disclosure of God and the means of human reconciliation with him… Vital also is the fact that Christian life should be the manifestation of a pervasive quality of love' (John Bowker, ed., Oxford, 2000, pp. 126-7).

The pervasive quality of supernatural love, typical of Christianity, means that as a religion involving more than a quarter of the world's population, Christianity could never be simply a collection of individuals concerned solely with their own individual salvation. On the contrary, despite shortcomings and failures, Christianity is a worldwide network of people who work together for a better world offering the salvation that comes from Jesus Christ.

It could be said that Christians form a collectivity that renders the risen Jesus Christ present in the world today. They allow him to journey again today among humanity, building it up in unity and universal fraternity. In that sense, it is Jesus himself more than simply his message that Christians want to give to the world.

The conviction that lies behind Christianity's missionary zeal is the belief that Jesus introduces the world to its true 'home', *the* Community of Communities: God, the Father, Son and Holy Spirit, three Divine Persons who love one another perfectly. Through Jesus' death and resurrection, God who is Love enables us to share in his own life, the source of happiness, peace, joy and dynamism. We become clothed in love.

In some ways, the implications of this central message of Christianity are only beginning to dawn on Christians. In essence, their religion wants to promote a vision of the world that is based on the realisation that we have only one God who is Father to us all and that we are all brothers and sisters of one another. Post 9/11, with the onset of world terrorism, Christians are coming to realise the extreme importance and contemporary relevance of their specific message.

The founding vision
One way to glimpse something of Jesus' vision would be to imagine what must have been going through his mind on the last night of his life on earth, the night before he died. What must he have thought as he recalled the years of childhood with Mary, Joseph and his cousins in Nazareth, and then the years of his public ministry with its successes and disappointments? What sentiments did he feel as he could see again in his mind's eye the crowds that followed him, the women that supported him, and the disciples that he had called? What must have darted through his heart as he thought about those whose lives had been transformed through meeting him and with whom he

had kept in contact as friends along his journey: Mary, Martha and Lazarus of Bethany, Mary of Magdala, Joanna, the wife of Chuza, steward of Herod Antipas...?

In the light of Jn 14-17, we can only guess that on the last night he must have considered again the vision he had held up to his followers, a vision so powerful that it attracted many, some radically. He had spoken of a 'kingdom', not a kingdom of this world, but a whole new world, one imbued with a recognition of the one God whom he called Father (*Abba* in Aramaic), and marked by new relationships between men and women, between rich and poor, between locals and foreigners, between people of different social categories, backgrounds and traditions.

During the three years of his public ministry he had looked on the crowds who had followed them. He had loved them as himself. He had wanted to set up bonds that would link them to him, and to one another.

Praying by night to heaven above and to the heaven within him, filled with light, Jesus had gone out day by day to those blind to the vision of God within them and around them and he offered them light.

To those who were dumb to the Word of God speaking within them, he spoke words of Truth so that they in turn would transmit to others his liberating, fulfilling and unifying words that would re-awaken people to *Life*.

To those who were paralysed, not knowing what God wanted of them, he spoke straight to their hearts urging them to enter into the eternal movement that is God-Infinite Love. And he showed that in this movement of love it holds true that by transmitting the fire of his vision and life, you yourself are set alight with a new burning fire within you.

And yet, despite his words of fire and truth, many people, even though they understood him, didn't want to understand, and decided to keep their eyes closed because their soul was dark. Jesus continued to look at them with love. He did not doubt. And so the night before he died, he summed up the whole of his mission in the prayer 'May they all be one'. Yes, just as he was united to God the Father in the Holy Spirit, he wanted his followers to be one and so be happy. Peace, happiness and fulfilment flow from the gift of his unity.

Was this 'founding vision' of Jesus a utopia? If it were only the inspiration of a human genius, it might have been. And it would have ended in failure. But since Jesus is divine-human, gave his life for this vision of unity, and rose from the dead, his founding vision didn't end up simply among the catalogues of wishful thinking. Christianity's central faith statement is: 'Jesus is risen' and lives among us. Jesus' founding vision lives on in the community that came to life out of his death and resurrection. As Dietrich Bonhoeffer put it: 'Jesus rose as community' and this community continues his founding vision.

The vision isn't simply a religious or 'spiritual' idea. While Jesus is truly God, it's vital to remember he is truly human. As perfectly human, Jesus summarised in himself all of humanity and all the truth about our human condition. His words and wisdom, his example and presence were directed towards making the concrete world we live in into a better place where peace and unity, justice and freedom, equality and diversity, fraternity and solidarity reign. The Christian community is, in a certain sense, a prolongation of his body now continuing this mission in the world.

Giving a soul to the world
Throughout the past two thousand years, the members and Churches of Christianity have contributed to the implanting of that founding vision in the socio-political contexts in which they lived. And it is always worth bearing in mind that Christians have lived through all kinds of political regimes – from empires to kingdoms, from tribes to republican nation states, from tyrannies to absolute rulers, from dictatorships to democracies!

Some expressions of Christianity haven't always lived up to the inspiring goal of the founder, but nevertheless, it is undeniable that the Christian family worldwide has built up a vast reservoir of experience, insight and, along the way, much self-discovery of what it means to be human in the light of Jesus Christ. He reveals both who God is, and who we are, since we are made in the image and likeness of God. It is the Gospel wisdom put into practice that Christianity wants to share with humanity today.

Undoubtedly, contemporary Christianity is witnessing a new search and a discovery of how best to communicate the Christian message. Jeanne Hinton of the Building Bridges of Hope project run by The Churches Together of Britain and Ireland has described the results of research she carried out among Christians recently by underlining what she calls 'a great yearning for relationship, for meaning and purpose, for honesty and authenticity, for justice and freedom, for community... a desire to deepen one's experience of God in a way that is life-giving and relevant to the world in which we live' (*Changing Churches*, CTBI, 2002, p. xii).

Christians know they need to have this experience of God in order to communicate God! A German theologian, Karl Rahner, along with others, has commented that Christians of the third millennium will either be mystic – have, and be able to relate, their 'experience' of God – or they simply won't be!

The point is that the founding vision of Christians isn't based on ritual or prayers or customs (although all of this is important), but rather the life they are called to live. An early third-century Christian, writing to his high-ranking pagan friend, Diognetus, who had asked for information about the religion of Christians, tells us as much. He gives us a pen-picture of how Christians understood their identity in terms of giving a soul, a life, and a vision to the world:

Christians are not distinguished from the rest of humankind by either country, speech, or customs; the fact is, they nowhere settle in cities of their own; they use no peculiar language; they cultivate no eccentric mode of life. Certainly, this creed of theirs is no discovery due to some conceit or speculation of inquisitive people; nor do they, as some sects do, champion any doctrine of human origin. Yet while they settle in both Greek and non-Greek cities, as each one's lot is cast, and conform to the customs of the country in dress, diet and mode of life in general, the whole tenor of their way of living stamps it as worthy of admiration and admittedly extraordinary... To say it briefly: what the soul is in the body, that the Christians are in the world. The soul is spread through all the members of the body, and the Christians throughout the cities of the world. The soul dwells in the body, but is not part and parcel of the body, so Christians dwell in the world, but are not part and parcel of the world. Itself invisible, the soul is kept shut up in the visible body; so Christians are known as such in the world, but their religion remains invisible... (Letter to Diognetus, quoted in J. Quasten, *Patrology Vol 1*, Westminster, Maryland: Newman Press, 1950, pp. 250-251).

Centuries have gone by since that text was written. And although Christianity today exists in a wide gamut of forms of community life, structures, movements, as well as social, artistic and cultural initiatives, the specific goal remains the same: that of uniting the one world family in God and for God, thereby giving the world's technological and global advances a 'soul'.

Re-discovering the founding vision: returning to origins

In all of religious and secular history one finds examples of moments when people, groups and communities wanted to get back again to their roots, to their origins. Often it happens when there's a crisis. A crisis is a situation where things hang in the balance, where old ways come to an end, but room for new possibilities open. It's a time for decision leading to new direction. At times of crisis people go back to the original vision because they want to go forward holding true to the original inspiring spark that gave rise to their initiative, group or organisation.

We see this desire to return to their origins in many people of Irish origin now living in America, England or Australia. They want to be in touch with their ancestral roots. How often have people in Ireland met visitors seeking to trace their roots, wanting to know where their family lived, who their relations might be, what the conditions were like when their relations left Ireland? It's important to them for their own self-identity.

On a more specific level, we can notice the pattern of return to origins in the Northern Ireland Peace Process. How often we have witnessed those involved return to the Good Friday Agreement to see what it was they all agreed upon or at least to examine again this foundational text in order to plot the way forward. This happens especially when there are crisis moments. People go back to the text and see in it the voice of the people, the majority of whom voted in favour of it. This text embodies the conclusion of a journey of dialogue that led up to it, so it contains the spirit, the principles, the objectives that people can look to as a roadmap for how to move forward from there.

After the horror of the destruction of World War II, the European Economic Community was established with a view to restoring stability, peace and economic prosperity. Recognising that a terrible vision of Europe had been pursued by Fascists and the Hitler regime, the founders of the new post-War Europe – Adenauer, De Gasperi, Monnet and Schumann – recalled the alternative vision of Europe, that based on an understanding of Europe whose origins lie in the marrying, especially in the light of Christianity, of the Greek/Roman /Celtic cultures, providing a rich tapestry of culture, vision and identity.

The whole point of setting up a new European union was to continue the European project that had been handed down from previous generations in a way that would guarantee fidelity to Europe's most noble ideals. Today too, in the newly extended Europe, there is a sense that we need to keep in touch with the Christian, Jewish and Islamic roots of Europe.

Recent events in the world of business speak of a return to origins taking place within economics. People talk of the climate of change in the post-Enron, or post-Parmalat contexts. Many in the business world are considering anew the origins and purpose of economics and business. Ethics has come back into fashion with people searching for a vision that will sustain business as directed towards the benefit of humanity and not humanity for the benefit of business.

Religious communities, too experience times when they return to their origins and start out again from there in the renewal of their religion. For instance, within Buddhism, the renewal movement of the Rissho Rosei-kai is one of the movements that seeks to renew Buddhism by highlighting Buddha's original message of altruism, peace and harmony with the universe.

The Christian 'return to origins'

Within Christianity the desire for contact with the origins is strong. Time and again throughout history, Christianity has witnessed moments when there has been a re-discovery of the founding vision of Jesus and the first Christian community. In recent times, too, many new movements and communities of renewal have come to life within the Catholic, Anglican, Protestant and Orthodox traditions. They help their members live a vibrant experience of the Gospel. We shall return to this in chapter five.

At this point, however, we want to note the pattern of return to origins within Christianity by examining some general features and then some specific instances from Christian history.

The first point to note is that Christianity is not a religion of the book only. Yes, the Bible is the Holy Book that recounts the founding vision. But the whole point is that the Christian vision is accompanied by the Visionary himself, the Founder of Christianity, Jesus Christ! Christians don't simply read about their past in their Holy Book as if they were reading a catalogue in a museum. Christian faith is a living 'today' reality.

The reason for this is the work of the Holy Spirit. The Spirit is the One who keeps Christianity as a living religion. The second century Christian theologian, Irenaeus, who was martyred in Lyons in France, called Jesus and the Holy Spirit, God the Father's 'two hands' who keep the vessel of the Christian community (the Church) ever young.

> [The faith transmitted by the Church] by the work of the Holy Spirit, like a precious deposit contained in a valuable vase, is ever rejuvenated and also rejuvenates the vase that contains it. To the Church, in fact, was entrusted the gift of God (cf. Jn 4:10) like the breath that is blown into the living being shaped from the soil of the ground (cf. Gen 2:7), so that all her members, by participating in it, are vivified by it; and in her has been deposited the communion with Christ, that is, the Holy Spirit... In fact, 'God has appointed, in the Church first apostles, second prophets, third teachers' (cf. 1 Cor 12:28) and imbued her with all the remaining operation of the Spirit (cf. 1 Cor 12:11)... For where the Church is, there too is the Spirit of God; and where the Spirit of God is, there too are the Church and every form of grace... (*Adversus Haereses* 3.14.1., ed. by A. Rousseau and L. Doutreleau, Sources Chrétiennes, vol. 211, Paris: Cerf, 1974, pp. 472-475)

More recently, in the twentieth century, the Orthodox Ecumenical Patriarch Athenagoras wrote: 'Without the Spirit,

God is far away, Christ remains in the past, the Gospel is a dead letter, the Church is a simple organisation, authority a domination, mission a propaganda, worship mere evocation, and Christian action a slave morality. But in the Spirit the Gospel is the power of life, the Church signifies Trinitarian communion, authority is a liberating service, mission is a Pentecost, the liturgy is memorial and anticipation, human activity is deified'. (Olivier Clément, *Dialogues avec le Patriarche Athénagoras*, Paris: Fayard, 1969, p. 496)

The Spirit has been active throughout the history of the Church, guaranteeing our contact with the origins of the Christian story in two ways.

Firstly, through sacraments and the preaching of the faith. The Apostles and their successors, the bishops, together with their collaborators, the priests and deacons, administer sacraments and preach the faith in Church. They do so in an institutional capacity as ordained ministers. In fact, St Augustine (354-430), one of the great intellectuals in the life of the Church, pointed out that the sacraments are efficacious regardless of the worthiness or otherwise of the bishop or priest.

In other words, from a Roman Catholic and Orthodox perspective, the risen Jesus Christ binds himself to the sacraments in such a way that when Mass is celebrated validly, the person receiving communion actually encounters the Risen Christ sacramentally present in the Eucharist. Likewise, in hearing the words of absolution at confession, the penitent is hearing the Risen Christ speak words of forgiveness and peace. So there is a 'guaranteed' presence of Jesus, the Origin of our religion, present in the sacraments.

But, alongside the sacraments and preaching of the faith, there is also what is called the charismatic or prophetic dimension of the Church. Throughout its history, the Church community has witnessed the emergence of numerous prophetic figures who cause the Gospel novelty to erupt again in each new era. We can think of a few names: Benedict,

Francis and Clare of Assisi, Catherine of Siena, Teresa of Avila, Ignatius of Loyola. Through these charismatic people, together with the communities they form, Christianity is brought into a renewed contact with the Gospel, opening up windows onto the Gospel that are appropriate for the new circumstances in which Christianity is to be lived out concretely. So, for example, Francis emphasised how we can live the whole Gospel from the perspective of poverty and this was very important for his era.

In a sense, therefore, the pattern of the Christian 'return to origins' is twofold. It comes about through sacraments and the preaching of the faith as well as through the Holy Spirit's action in providing prophetic impulses along the Church's journey. In Christianity, the return to origins is not simply a case of remembering the past more vividly. Since Jesus is risen and the whole of the world's history is in his hands, he is calling us to work with him and move towards him. He promised to be with us until the end of time (Mt 28:20).

The Christian return to origins is, paradoxically, also a movement to the future. Since Jesus contains all time, including the future, he is drawing us, like a magnet, towards our fulfilment in him. As well as being the beginning point for Christians, Jesus is also the end point. That is why, drawing on the first and last letters of the Greek alphabet, the author of the Book of Revelation called Jesus the 'Alpha' and the 'Omega'. He is our beginning and our end.

So our return to origins is a going forward to what we were originally meant to be in God's plan: totally united with the whole world reconciled in Jesus Christ. And he who is our origin and our end has promised to be with us along our journey: 'For where two or three are gathered in my name, I am there among them' (Mt 18:20). Jesus Christ is alive and travels with us so that in opening up the past to us again (i.e. helping us rediscover the Gospel with new eyes), through the work of the Holy Spirit, Jesus inspires enthusiasm in us and propels us not backwards but forwards.

Let us now examine the pattern of returning to origins in Christianity in the case of a number of examples.

The Céilí Dé

Christianity arrived in Ireland around 432. We know that monasticism was of huge significance in the first centuries of Christianity on the island of Ireland. Communities of monks literally dotted the Irish landscape, presenting a vibrant face of the Church that attracted so many friends and neighbours that the monastery became almost like a diocese in its extension and impact. Monasticism itself was a current of renewal within Christianity that had begun in the desert in Egypt and spread throughout Europe. Ireland, therefore, benefited straightaway from the arrival of a renewed and renewing life of Christianity.

Since 'the great monasteries were the indispensable framework of the Christian church in Ireland' (Patrick Corish, *The Irish Catholic Experience: A Historical Survey*, Dublin: Gill and MacMillan, 1985, p. 13), it is also true to say that the monasteries helped shape Irish culture. The Abbots wielded enormous influence and people in the locality had a sense of belonging to a particular monastic region. The monasteries became centres of learning, worship, healing and missionary outreach.

The Monastic movement or renewal did great good not only in Ireland, but also throughout Europe. However, it's also true that the monastic communities themselves needed every now and then to be reformed! In the eighth century there were many reform movements in the Western Church. Ireland too was in need of this renewal. In fact, one can read of various abuses, not to mention battles, between monasteries, as well as armed conflicts between monasteries and local princes. Hardly an ideal situation for Christian communities!

In the mid eighth century a reform movement began in Ireland, the leaders of which called themselves 'Céilí Dé'. A rough translation of this Irish term would be 'Servants of God' (the Anglicisation of this expression is 'Culdees'). They wanted to bring about renewal of the monastic life in Ireland.

The Céilí Dé was a movement of people that felt a strong calling to put God first in their lives and make themselves true servants or clients of God. No matter how important the abbot or the monastery, other people, family, possessions or their own lives might be, it was more important to choose God as their all in life. It seems this movement may have come from abroad, but it took root and developed in Ireland in its own way. Mael Ruáin (d. 792) of Tallaght is the one most associated with the beginnings of this current of renewal, but its radical nature can be seen in the establishment of isolated foundations such as Sceilig Mhíchíl off the Kerry coast.

It is not easy to sum up the ideals of these reformers who also called themselves 'sons of life'. The spirituality and way of life of the Céilí Dé is best known to us from three related texts: *The Monastery of Tallaght Text*; *The Rule of Tallaght;* and *The Rule of the Céilí Dé.*

The renowned historian, Professor Corish, provides a good brief outline of what characterised them: 'Essentially they called for a renewal of the ancient ascetic tradition, with special emphasis on study and the anchoretic or hermit life. The devotional literature of the Culdees is very distinctively Irish, with its imaginative freshness and its constant repetition of phrases expressing trust and abandonment... Above all, this spirituality expressed itself in highly personal religious poetry...' (Corish, p. 22). Indeed, the Céilí Dé movement in the Church generated a considerable literature, in particular in the monasteries of Tallaght and Finglas. Much of the early Irish nature poetry is attributed to them.

The Céilí Dé spirituality attributed great importance to the Word of God. Gospels were read at mealtime. It is said that a certain Adamnán succeeded in calming monastic troubles in far-off Clonmacnois by raising the Gospel. Afterwards, he said that 'the sign of the Cross by the power of the Gospel travels quicker than the wink of an eye... and vanishes every obstacle' (see Michael Maher, *Irish Spirituality*, Dublin: Veritas, 1981, p. 30). The epistles of St Paul and Gospel of St John were given special prominence.

The development of the Céilí Dé movement was not uniform. It was a current of renewal rather than a movement setting up new structures. Though critical of the laxity and secularisation they saw in the monasteries around them, the Céilí Dé didn't establish new monasteries. Rather they set to work to reform the monastic movement from within. In the monasteries at Tallaght and Finglas, 'the two eyes of Ireland' as they were called, all the monks were Céilí Dé. In others they lived the life of anchorites or hermits within the monastery.

They were very much devoted to the saints and hagiography was very important for them. They promoted recognition of Patrick as a 'national' figure and they encouraged devotion to him.

Although the central weakness of this reform movement was that it lacked structure, the Céilí Dé were interested in the general pastoral mission of the monasteries. They brought a new spirit rather than new structures, but this new spirit bore good fruits. They worked to ensure that there were more and better-educated priests. They concerned themselves with the observance of Sunday as a day of rest.

The Céilí Dé underlined the importance of following the guidance of one's *'anam chara'* or 'soul friend'. Mael Ruáin saw it of great importance. It was through the context of soul friendship that private confession took root in the Irish Church and later spread throughout Western Christendom. Christianity moved forward renewed by this wave of renewed life that had blown through the Church at that time. It was the fruit of the Gospel origins of Christianity rediscovered.

Mendicant orders

The 'mendicant orders' are so called because the word 'mendicant', meaning begging, best suited the poverty and humility characteristic of the new orders that sprang into life in the thirteenth centuries. They were founded by inspiring figures such as Francis of Assisi (1181-1226) and Dominic Guzman (c. 1170-1221).

These new Movements emerged at a time when Christian Europe was going through what has been called the 'Autumn of the Medieval Age' as Europe was entering into the modern era. Feudal structures were in decline and cities were beginning to emerge. Because of increased commercial activity and also because of the Crusades, new contacts were opening up between cities and regions, both in the West and in the East. The new social context needed something more than the older types of monasteries and Church structures that had been developing in the previous centuries.

The Church was facing various problems. It was becoming quite bourgeois and wealthy. Many of the clergy were uneducated and taken up with the privileges and money the older feudal structures gave them. Classical philosophical texts were discovered through contact with the Arab world and this posed intellectual challenges for the Church. Universities were coming to life.

It was at this time too that the Albigensian heresy was spreading. This was a form of Manichaeism that emphasised a dualism of a good god and an evil god. With its negative view of the body and the world, the Albigensian heresy, along with others at this time, preached an austere asceticism. These heresies rejected the Church and sacraments. While wanting the Church to be poorer (in itself a good thing), some heretical movements came to life at this time with a very anticlerical stance.

It was at this time that the Mendicant movements began in the Church. They were made up of people who, full of ideals and holy ambition, wanted to fight for Christ. What was distinctive about them, however, was that they didn't want to go off and separate themselves from the people, but rather share in the people's joys and sufferings. Secondly, they did love poverty as a witness to authentic Christianity, but they also wanted to spread the truth through preaching and lead many people to the Church. The Mendicant orders enriched the Church with a desire to return to the Gospel. The 'charisms' or 'gifts' given to Dominic, Francis and other mendicants by the Holy Spirit were soon seen as a response of God to the Church to help her at that critical time.

Francis of Assisi and Dominic Guzman, as well as others, emerged as major prophetic characters pointing to new ways forward for the Church. Each had a different message, but each had a unique role in bringing about a renewal in the life of the Church. Soon many people were following them as their 'children' in the charism that God was sending for that time. There was something fresh, alive, and novel about them and people felt drawn to this. The founders of the Mendicant Orders began to emphasise the importance of living the Gospel radically without 'ifs' or 'buts'.

Francis of Assisi (1181-1226)
Francis came from a wealthy family in Assisi. A number of events prepared him for the discovery of his vocation in the Church.

Firstly, he was injured during one of the many battles that took place between rival cities. Secondly, one day upon meeting a leper on the road he instinctively drew back, but then managed to control his natural aversion and embraced the leper, giving him all the money he had. Thirdly, he made a pilgrimage to Rome and seeing the miserly offerings at the tomb of St Peter, he emptied his purse and gave all he had. Next he exchanged his fine clothes for those of a tattered beggar man and stood for the rest of the day fasting among the horde of beggars at the door of the basilica. Not long after his return to

Assisi, while Francis was praying before an ancient crucifix in the abandoned and rundown wayside chapel of St Damian's below the town, he heard a voice saying: 'Go, Francis, and repair my house, which as you see is falling into ruin'. He took this seriously and started selling what he had to raise funds.

A major turning point came, however, when one day at Mass he was struck by the Gospel of the day recounting the episode from Jesus' life when he sent out his disciples telling them they were to possess neither gold nor silver, nor to carry two coats, shoes, or a staff, and that they were to exhort sinners to repentance and announce the Kingdom of God. Francis took these words as if spoken directly to himself, and as soon as Mass was over he cast away what he had left of his world's goods, his shoes, cloak, pilgrim staff, and empty wallet. At last he had found his vocation.

Despite all the initial reaction on the part of his family and many of his townspeople, soon others were following Francis in a radical following of Jesus. Among them was Clare of Assisi. Around both Francis and Clare a new spiritual family or movement came to life in the Church. The feature of this Franciscan spirituality was to live the whole Gospel from the perspective of poverty. Poverty was their window onto the Gospel.

Dominic Guzman (c. 1170-1221)
The founder of the Friars Preachers, as the Dominicans are known, was born of a Castilian family. In 1206 the turning point of his life came when his bishop, Diego, became unofficial leader of a papal mission to the heretical Albigensians. The bishop chose Dominic as his companion and they formed a community characterised by simplicity and poverty. They undertook discussions with their opponents for which they prepared very carefully.

Dominic had to live through five years of a terrible civil war with much massacre and savagery. But he and his followers persevered in their mission of converting the Albigensians by persuasion addressed to the heart and mind. In 1215 he established a headquarters in Toulouse, and the idea of an order of preachers began to take shape.

Dominic's intuition was to set up a body of highly trained priests on a monastic basis. It would be important to them to hand on what it is they had contemplated in their life of prayer, solitude and study. To that end, just like in monasteries, they would be bound by vows, especially poverty. But they wouldn't be bound to the monastery itself. They would devote themselves to the active work of preaching and teaching anywhere and everywhere.

Dominic's initiative was formally approved at Rome in 1216. One year later he sent eleven of his brothers, over half the then total, to the University of Paris and to Spain. Dominic travelled tirelessly, building up the new order and preaching as he went. One of the features of Dominic's mission was the importance he put on the help of women in his work.

If Francis opened up the Gospel for the people of his time through the window of poverty, it could be said that Dominic opened up the same Gospel, but this time through the window of Truth. The one Gospel, different windows, each one valid and enriching for those who were attracted by God to follow these charismatic figures of that time in history.

People were attracted to the novelty of these new Mendicant communities. They exhibited many similar features. For instance, often the communities were made up of lay brothers and priests living a common life together. The members of these orders were out and about preaching the Gospel and involved in the debates of the time.

People wanted to hear the Gospel and not just attend the rituals on Sunday. Soon itinerant preachers were to be found in many places, corresponding to the need for evangelisation and combating heretical movements by proposing an experience of true life: that of the Gospel lived in a community of brothers in obedience to the Church.

The brothers in these communities offered their preaching, sacraments and spiritual assistance to those who needed it. Money wasn't an issue. They themselves shared their goods and lived a communion of goods. They simply 'begged' when in need. Their poverty became a sign and a prophecy in a world in which commerce, wealth and monetary well-being were becoming the hallmarks of what it meant to be human. The brothers of these Mendicant orders welcomed all who wanted to follow Christ in their fraternity without questioning the social background of those who applied to join them.

What mattered was their fraternity in Christ. Soon these Mendicant Orders were like a network of fraternities, companies of friends for whom the one Lord was Christ and the one goal in life was to give him glory. Life in community was vital for them. A person could be a bishop, a professor, an advisor to the Pope, and yet he was dressed and ate the same as every other one of the brothers with whom he lived. Poverty was lived not as an end in itself, but as the means to be equal and be in communion with the other brothers of the convent.

Their poverty also meant Gospel freedom and total availability for the mission. They could travel and not have to worry so much about the upkeep of a big monastery. The model in all of this, of course, was the early Christian community in Jerusalem as described in the Acts of the Apostles.

The members in the Mendicant Orders took the Gospel to heart and so they went out 'two by two' as Jesus had commanded. They went out to preach the 'Gospel of mission' as Francis used to say. Their common life together was both the witness to the Gospel and the methodology for its proclamation.

By travelling around the 'brothers' broke down barriers between city-states and groups and promoted fraternity. If the former monasteries had provided stability in Europe at a time when migrations were a big problem (after the collapse of the

Roman Empire), now these new fraternities were responding to the need to open people up to others as brothers and sisters in other city-states so often locked in conflict.

For all of these reasons, the Mendicant Orders soon became very significant at the cultural level of European civilisation. They brought new life to the Continent. They also contributed much to the universities, as we can see from the examples of Albert the Great and Thomas Aquinas. The current of renewal they brought influenced artists such as Giotto and Beato Angelico and literary figures such as Dante. Soon economics too was to be influenced by the Franciscan philosophy.

The new movements were not initially accepted with enthusiasm by all. Unlike the older monasteries generally isolated in the country, the members of these new fraternities were living side by side with everyone in the cities. Jealousies soon became part of the picture, even among bishops and priests in local dioceses and parishes. But the Popes sensed their importance and gave them a series of privileges, above all, placing them under the Pope's own protection.

The story is told of Pope Innocent III having a dream in which he saw the main cathedral in Rome, St John Lateran, about to fall down. It didn't fall because it was supported by the simple, poor, Francis of Assisi. The Pope interpreted his dream to mean that Francis and his followers would renew the Church.

The emergence of the Mendicant Orders was one of those moments of the return to the Gospel origins of the Church that brought a new injection of life into Christianity.

Martin Luther
The story of Martin Luther (1483-1546) provides us with a direct example of someone whose very name is immediately associated with the word 'reform' in the Church. He was born at Eisleben, Germany, and educated at Erfurt and Magdeburg. Initially he thought of becoming a lawyer, but

after a near-death experience he decided to become an Augustinian monk.

Through his theology studies, Luther became very familiar with the style of theology of the Middle Ages. He began to teach the Bible at the University of Wittenberg where he lectured on the Psalms as well as St Paul's letters to the Romans, to the Galatians and the Letter to the Hebrews.

While professor in Wittenberg, Martin Luther went through a very dark period where he struggled with the issue of his own salvation. His basic question was: 'How can I find a merciful God?' He went through an experience of such tribulation that it was akin to hell for him. He described it as follows: 'I know a man who is certain he underwent sufferings of this sort on several occasions. They lasted only for a very short time, but were so oppressive and infernal that no language could have expressed them, no pen could have described them, no inexperienced person could have believed them. They were such that if they had reached their greatest intensity or lasted only half an hour, the man would have inevitably died and all his bones would have been reduced to ashes... In that moment, the soul cannot believe it will one day be redeemed' (Weimarer Ausgabe 1, 557f., Resolutions on the 95 Theses). This dark experience arose from that deep contradiction in all of us that St Paul describes in the letter to the Romans: 'I do not do the good I want, but the evil I do not want is what I do' (Rom 7:19).

Having closely studied St Paul and having had this experience, Luther regarded it as certain that no one could overcome this contradiction on their own. However, he didn't mean, as is often thought he meant, that it's impossible for us to avoid doing wrong. The problem for Luther was much more complex. What Luther saw was that instead of doing the good only out of love and with absolute selflessness, even when we do good, there's ultimately always a secret tendency in us to do what we're doing for our own good. In a word, we're afflicted by a 'curvature', a turning back on ourselves that hides itself even under the most noble of motives and actions.

And this is what Luther saw as the real dilemma, since none of us can free ourselves from this tendency. Even if you tried to do it, in order to be just and holy, this again would be selfish and fall back into what, for Luther, would be 'sin' in the full sense of the word.

What happens when you notice this tendency? You understand that you are truly fallen, and this brings with it the danger of deep despair, because you know what God wants of you and accept it, but you aren't able to carry it out to the end. You are not able to love God and your neighbour with your whole heart. So you end up seeing yourself as irrevocably lost and you experience then the tremendous wrath of God. And this is what Luther means by 'tribulation.'

At a certain point, however, during his years of anxious searching, Luther began to see that this is only one aspect of Christianity. God is not only a judge. He hasn't only given us the law. There's a whole other aspect of the Christian message, the Gospel, and it really is Good News. Luther began to see that precisely there when you're at zero point and don't know what to do, God does not reject you forever, as you might think, but bends down towards your weakness and nothingness and recreates you. He does this on one condition: that you believe, that is, that you abandon yourself to him with complete trust.

This was Luther's great and liberating discovery. If God were just in terms of the human justice of 'give that you may receive', we'd have no chance before him. But God and his justice are not like that. God does not take account only of our injustice, our selfishness, our slight holiness and our little love, and treat us as we deserve. Rather, he is there, ready to make up for our nothingness and to communicate his own being, his holiness and justice, thus making of us 'new people'. In his famous Heidelberg Disputation of April 26, 1518, Luther writes: 'God's love does not find [in the world] what he loves, but he creates it.' And that's what makes God's love different from ours, which is 'attracted by what is lovable.'

Luther himself writes about this discovery in the famous autobiographical fragment of 1545: 'Then I began to understand the justice of God as that justice by which the just man lives by God's gift and precisely by faith... As it is written, "The just man lives by faith." [Rom 1:17] Here I felt as if I were completely reborn and as if I had entered through the wide-opened gates of Paradise itself. Immediately there, all of Scripture showed me a different countenance'.

Luther went on to emphasise the individual freedom that comes through faith. For Luther, the Christian is the most free of all creatures and so the most dutiful of all by helping others to become 'Christs to one another'. Rooted in Christ, the Christian has to become a 'Christ' for his neighbour. But this is not a burden made up of duties or tasks to be fulfilled on our own efforts. On the contrary, he saw it as God's gift (grace) alone that enables us to follow Jesus Christ. Luther focused on faith as the way to know God and not reason. For him it was Scripture and not so much the Church teaching that mattered. Hence we get three famous principles associated with Luther: *sola scriptura, sola fide, sola gratia* (scripture alone, faith alone, grace alone).

On the basis, therefore, both of his Scripture studies and personal experiences, Luther reacted against practices which he considered had no foundation in Scripture and were merely manmade – indulgences, some of the sacraments, praying for the dead, the position of the Pope. His personal experience led him to see the Church not as a hierarchical structure, but merely as a spiritual community and he promoted the priesthood of all believers. In subsequent developments he lost sight of the fact that Church teaching, sacraments, and practices help us abandon ourselves to God, and are themselves gifts from God enabling us to respond fully to God.

On the basis of his discovery and his desire to return to the origins of the Church in the Gospel, Luther's desire was to reform, not split, the Church. He hoped for a general council to resolve the issues. He outlined the foundations of his new theology in five treatises published between May and November 1520: *Treatise of Good Works; The Papacy at Rome; Address to the German Nobility; Babylonian Captivity of the Church; Freedom of a Christian Man.*

Martin Luther's reform occurred just after the printing press was invented. The bible was distributed like never before. Luther saw the printing press as 'God's latest and best work to spread the true religion'. His translation of the Bible into German became important for the German Language. Soon the reformation brought with it huge socio-political upheaval that reshaped the face of Europe.

Lutherans themselves readily admit Luther's limitations. Unfortunately, Luther's experience, instead of being a gift to the Church, also became a point of division. It cannot be denied that in Luther's experience there was something very new in relation to the prevailing understanding of Christianity at that time, something too new to be easily received and too new also perhaps for him to be able to propose it to others in a fully balanced manner.

On a number of occasions, Pope John Paul II has commented positively on Luther's religious passion, his request for a theology that was nearer to Scripture and his call to the reform of the Church. Citing Pope Adrian VI who in 1522 attempted to launch a renewal programme for the Church in response to the Lutheran reform, the Pope has spoken of the need for Catholics to seek a new evaluation of the many issues raised by Luther and his message.

The Evangelical Movement in early nineteenth-century Protestantism

The early nineteenth century was a time of a great 'Evangelical Awakening', a Movement or current of renewal that swept through different Churches in different countries. It involved returning to some key doctrines of the sixteenth-century Reformers – Scripture alone as sufficient for teaching the way of salvation, the prevenient character of divine grace, justification by faith, the priesthood of all believers.

A major feature of the Evangelical Movement was pietistic fervour. It highlighted the subjective aspect of faith as well as the emotional, felt experience of one's faith. It emphasised conversion followed by the sanctifying of one's religious affections.

Ruth Rouse points out that, whatever its origins, '...its spirit and its underlying motives were always the same. Its passion was evangelism – evangelism at home and to the ends of the earth. One result of this passion was in evidence everywhere – the coming into being of societies, voluntary movements, or organisations, in which Christians of different Churches and different nations banded themselves together to win the world for Christ. The compelling impulse that drew them together was the sense, born of their personal experience of salvation, that all people everywhere have need of Christ. As redeemed, they had a mission to proclaim redemption' (Ruth Rouse and Stephen C. Neill, eds., *A History of the Ecumenical Movement I*, Geneva, WCC, 1993, p. 309).

The new wave of enthusiasm, commitment and missionary zeal across the Protestant Churches in the early nineteenth century didn't come out of the blue. In Germany, it can be traced back to the Pietist movement in the eighteenth century. In Britain the Evangelical Renewal came largely, though not totally, from the evangelistic efforts of the Wesleys and Whitefield and the rise of Methodism. In America it followed the Great Awakening of the eighteenth century and the response of the Churches to the spiritual needs of the frontier.

Though prepared for, the Evangelical Movement brought new winds of missionary zeal. Indeed, it has been said that 'No outburst of missionary zeal, unless it be the Jesuit Mission of the 16th century, has ever paralleled the missionary developments resulting from the Evangelical Awakening between 1790 and 1820' (Rouse, p. 310). Many Missionary societies were established to send out missionaries to countries where the message of Jesus Christ had not yet been preached. Coupled with their missionary zeal outwards, the early leaders of the Evangelical Awakening also engaged in a stringent attack on social evils at home. With missionary zeal here too, the leaders expressed their concern in the Lord's name for the bodies as well as the souls of others. Temperance and purity movements as well as peace societies came into being.

The Evangelical Movement led eventually in 1846 to the formation of 'The Evangelical Alliance' of Christian individuals of different Churches who shared evangelical principles. This ecumenical organisation produced remarkable and far-reaching results. It stimulated united prayer, held international conferences, became a powerful instrument of international Christian education and a powerful advocate of Missions, as well as a defender of religious liberty.

In time, the Evangelical Movement led to the creation of new denominations within the Church of Christ. Methodism, the earliest form of Evangelical Awakening, eventually became a distinct Church (the formal split from the Anglican Communion coming in 1891). The Awakening in Switzerland and France contributed to the formation of Free Churches in several Swiss cantons and in France. It was the Evangelical ministers in the Church of Scotland, with their emphasis on spiritual freedom of the Church, who founded the Free Church of Scotland in 1843.

Paul Avis summarises the situation in England as follows: 'Evangelicalism was divided between Anglicans touched by the evangelical revival who remained within the structures of the Church of England, and Methodists who eventually moved away to form an independent ecclesial tradition, though with strong roots in Anglican theology and liturgy' (Paul Avis, *Anglicanism and the Christian Church*, London: T&T Clark, 2002, p. 157).

One unintentional but very positive development was that the leaders of the Evangelical Movement became pioneers of the movement for Christian Unity that was to come later in the nineteenth century and early in the twentieth. The reason for this was that the Evangelical Awakening led to active co-operation between members of Protestant Churches. Through it Christians joined together in international Christian dialogue and action, missionary awakening, and efforts directed to social reform. Even though each of the new societies and movements that came to life out of the Evangelical Movement had its own specific missionary work or social reform to promote, nevertheless, albeit unconsciously, all of them together began to create a sense of togetherness among Christians of different Churches.

Vatican II

The Second Vatican Council was the religious event of the twentieth century (1962–65). Summoned by the charismatic Pope John XXIII, one of the most loved people of his generation, the Council set out to update and to renew the Catholic Church and her mission to the world. The inspiring example was that of the early Christian community.

In the words of Rosemary Goldie, one of the women observers at the Council, it was 'the point of both arrival and departure for renewal in the life of the Catholic Church, and a significant landmark for the Christian world as a whole' (*From a Roman Window*, London: HarperCollins, 1998, p. 3).

Both John XXIII and Pope Paul VI who brought the Council to a conclusion after four lengthy sessions, focused the 3,000 bishops of the world on listening to the promptings of the Holy Spirit in order to hear anew the voice of Christ, the Shepherd of the Church and the Saviour of the world. Lay Catholic observers (13 men and 13 women) as well as observers from other Churches (100 delegated observers as well as other guests) and even a representative of the world religions (Nikko Nirwano, founder of the Rissho Kosei-kai, a Buddhist renewal movement) were present at the deliberations of the Council.

The tone and the attitude of the Council can be caught in the following quote from the opening paragraph of the Constitution on Divine Revelation, '...the present Council wishes to set forth authentic teaching about divine revelation... so that by hearing the message of salvation the whole world may believe, by believing it may hope, and by hoping it may love.'

The Council, the twenty-first in the history of the Church, looked out over the landscape of the modern world to offer the men and women of our times a reason to live, a reason to hope and a reason to love. But for that to happen, it was necessary to go back again to the founding vision of Jesus.

'Jesus Christ is the light of the world' are the words with which the Council opened its constitution on the Church. When this light shines into the hearts of men and women, they find meaning and purpose and happiness, for 'the truth is that it is only in the mystery of the incarnate Word the mystery of what it is to be human takes on light' (*Pastoral Constitution on the Church in the Modern World*, 22).

The Council listened with two ears, as it were: with one, it listened again to the voice of the Risen Lord and the Good News in order to start again from the Gospel, launching a re-evangelisation of all in the Church. With the other ear, it listened to 'the joys and the hopes, the griefs and the anxieties of the people of this age, especially those who are poor or in any way afflicted' (*Pastoral Constitution on the Church in the Modern World*, 1), explaining that these are also the concerns of the followers of Christ.

The central conviction running throughout the programme of renewal launched by the Council was that while the substance of the Faith does not change, for it is 'the faith given once for all to the saints' (Jude 3), its dress, how it is expressed, needs to be updated in order for the Church to speak to the men and women of today. Indeed, *'aggiornamento'* became one of the catchwords of that time.

The Council pointed up what might be called 'the sources of God'. These sources are the inspired Scriptures, the sacraments as 'the source and summit' of our Faith, and the mutual love between Christians (Mt 18:20). Its aim was to root the Church more deeply in her divine sources in order to send her out to renew the face of the earth. For this is always the task of the Church – not to attempt a mere modification of humankind and the world but rather a profound renewal bringing the Kingdom of God. History will belong to those who love.

The Council, in short, inspired four great dialogues which now activate the post-Conciliar Church's mission to the world: the dialogue among Catholics; the ecumenical dialogue with Christians of other Churches and communities; the dialogue with the great religions of the world; and the dialogue with all people of good will who aspire to building up a more united, just and humane world. This is so much the case that Pope John Paul II repeats the principle that dialogue is the way of the Catholic Church for our times.

Liberation Theology

For the past one hundred years or so, the Church has increasingly focused on the social dimension of redemption. To say we are saved means that, through Jesus Christ, we have been brought into a right relationship with God and have been enabled to love our neighbour in a Gospel manner.

In 1968 a Second General Conference of Latin American Bishops in Medellin spoke of an 'option for the poor'. After this meeting, Gustavo Gutiérrez' book, *A Theology of Liberation: History, Politics and Salvation*, reflected on how sin and salvation refer not only to individual personal realities but also to social structures. He proposed a method for doing theology called a 'critical reflection on praxis'.

Starting from the paradigm of liberation that runs throughout the Bible, Gutiérrez proposed the starting point for reflection had to be the lived experience of those in situations of poverty and marginalisation. It was, after all, in the context of the slavery in Egypt that the Exodus occurred, the great event when people came to know God as their liberator and Covenant-partner, the One who gives the commandments as a way of life. The event of Jesus' death and resurrection speaks of liberation from all situations of oppression and social slavery.

On the basis of Gutiérrez's theology of liberation, others began to apply his method by reflecting not only on situations of economic poverty but taking various forms of marginalisation as a starting point.

Two Vatican Documents (1984 and 1986), while confirming this new direction in theology called 'liberation theology', also pointed out possible doctrinal deviations, not least the confusion that would arise by adopting Marxist categories as a framework for theological reflection.

Many of the insights of the theology of liberation have now been integrated into mainstream theology. Increasingly, the social and liberation aspect of the Church's teaching has been highlighted.

1.2   JESUS AND HIS MESSAGE IN CONTEMPORARY CULTURE

European art, architecture, music and literature of the past two thousand years have been shaped largely by Christianity. Well-known examples come readily to mind and information on all of these can be found on the internet:
- the wall paintings on stone coffins and slabs in the catacombs of Rome such as the Good Shepherd images;
- the distinctive Irish High Crosses such as Muiredach's Cross found in Monasterboice, Co. Louth;
- The Book of Kells;
- the majestic sculpture reliefs of the great cathedrals such as Notre Dame in Paris or Rheims Cathedral with their

presentation of the world as understood in Christian doctrine (heaven, earth, purgatory and hell);
- the famous windows of Chartres with their biblical scenes;
- Michelangelo's *Pietà* in St Peter's Basilica, Rome;
- Caravaggio's *The Taking of Christ* that hangs in the National Gallery in Dublin;
- Handel's Messiah first performed in Dublin;
- Christian epics such as 'Beowulf' and 'Paradise Lost'.
- Literature such as the novels of the Russian writers Fyodor Dostoevsky and Leo Tolstoy as well as the Spaniard Miguel de Unamuno's poetry and prose.

In the second millennium especially, cultural expressions often revolved around direct images of, or references to, Jesus, Mary, the saints and episodes from the Gospel. A record of the works of art, depicting images of Christ throughout the centuries, was put together in the year 2000 by Neil MacGregor in a documentary series entitled *Seeing Salvation* (video, BBCV, 7179).

Apart from direct images of Jesus, much of Europe's creative energy has also been inspired by Christian motifs such as vicarious redemption, forgiveness, the goodness of creation, faith, resurrection of the body, heaven, and the centrality of charity. An analysis of this influence on modern European literature has been put together by Daniel Murphy in his work entitled *Christianity and Modern European Literature* (Dublin: Four Courts, 1997).

One of the great challenges, however, facing Christianity as it enters the third millennium is the split that has come about between the Gospel and culture, between faith and its expression in the everyday lives of people. And this is true also in the realms of the arts in general. Be that as it may, images of Jesus are not lacking in the contemporary culture of music and art, film and literature.

Film

There are many works such as Roy Kinnard and Tim Daly's *Divine Images: A History of Jesus on the Screen* (1992, Citadel Press) that have traced the range of films depicting Jesus throughout the past one hundred years since the invention of moving pictures in the 1890s. The first 'Jesus' film was *The Passion Play at Oberammergau* (1898), but the hundred-year history includes such well-know films as Franco Zeffirelli's *Jesus of Nazareth*, Denys Arcand's *Jesus of Montreal*, Scorsese's *The Last Temptation of Christ*, Andrew Lloyd Webber's *Jesus Christ Superstar* and DeMille's *King of Kings* (see http://post.queensu.ca/~rsa/realreel.htm; *The Journal of Religion and Film* can also be accessed on line). Each film has its own image of Jesus and not without controversy! He is depicted in so many ways – as a hippie, as an unflappable reserved character, as a model of detachment, as a tormented wonderer, as a dreamer, and as a hero.

Among the more classic examples of films with a Christian theme those directed by Krzysztof Kieslowski, Olmi and Andrey Tarkovsky deserve mention. Here, however, we shall look at the Italian, Pier Paolo Pasolini's, *The Gospel According to Matthew*. It is regarded as something of a modern classic. Pasolini, a Marxist, was fascinated with the person of Jesus Christ and his Gospel of poverty that Pasolini considered still unknown to so many.

In terms of text, Pasolini's film is the purest of the 'Jesus' films in the sense that it takes Matthew's Gospel and uses this straight text throughout the film. Special effects are kept to a minimum. Hand-held cameras are used to get a realistic documentary 'you are there' feel. In addition, Pasolini keeps to a stark black and white cinematography. However, he adopts an inventive use of music that ranges from Bach to Congolese song and on to Billie Holliday.

In Pasolini's film, Jesus is portrayed as an outcast, driven by anger at social injustice. In fact, Enrique Arazoqui, the non-professional who played the part of Jesus, was himself a leftist

Spanish economics student. Christ comes across as a stern revolutionary, preaching a Gospel of the poor to the poor. It has been said that this message of poverty was inspired by Pope John XXIII, himself anything but stern (!), who had died shortly before the movie was made and to whom Pasolini dedicated the film because of this Pope's simplicity and love of the poor.

More recently, Mel Gibson has produced *The Passion of the Christ*. In some ways, films such as *The Passion of the Christ*, depicting the episodes linked to the death of Jesus, are reminiscent of the Medieval Passion Play tradition. The image of Jesus that comes across is that of the suffering saviour of the world. It is the physical wounds of Jesus that are highlighted. By his wounds we have been healed and saved.

Gibson was motivated to produce this film because of a strong personal sense of salvation. He recalls a time when he found himself trapped with feelings of terrible, isolated emptiness, regret and despair. He had been neglecting his faith for about eighteen years. Through a retreat experience, however, he turned once again to God in prayer and found a new confidence in the realisation that Jesus had taken away all our sins on the Cross. It was this conviction that inspired him to present the redemptive, passionate love of Jesus laying down his life for us.

Art

Apart from films, there are many whose work in the visual arts indicates the influence of Christianity: Andy Warhol's later works and the works of Marc Chagall, Stanley Spencer, Mark Rothko, Barnett Newman, Hughie O'Donoghue, Mainie Jellet, Evie Hone and Imogen Stuart.

Georges Rouault, a French artist, made the face of Jesus the great subject of his art. He is widely considered the most important Christian religious artist of the twentieth century. Born during the French army's siege of the Paris Commune,

Rouault also witnessed World War I. It was a time of seeing just what people could do to each other if left on their own.

Moving from his early expressionistic work to his mature iconlike paintings of Jesus, he attempted to present an image of Jesus in today's world. He depicted Jesus among the poor, the destitute and the proletariat life in Paris. His imagery of Jesus was an attempt to recover his message for our day and also re-propose old art forms in a new guise. While Jesus is depicted as tortured he never appears defeated by sin, but rather is meek and compassionate.

Mainie Jellett was born in Dublin into a Church of Ireland family. Developing as a Cubist painter, she became a leading figure of modern art in Ireland. A believer throughout her life, what 'mattered essentially to Jellett was faith in her art, and faith in and a personal relationship with Christ which she could find and live amongst friends of different denominations and beliefs in a truly ecumenical spirit' (Gesa E. Thiessen, *Theology and Modern Irish Art,* Dublin: Columba Press, 1999, p. 40).

Various motifs from Christianity are to be found in her works. Among them, the theme of the Crucified Christ as portrayed in *The Ninth Hour,* a depiction of the Crucified Christ with John and Mary at the foot of the Cross (Hugh Lane Municipal Gallery of Modern Art, Dublin). This painting seems to lead us into a spiritual universe in which the faceless (and so perhaps taking on every face), crucified Jesus is the entrance door. Again this work of art reflected the centrality of the artist's image of Jesus based on her faith. The crucified God is important for Jellett. It is said that each Good Friday she attended the commemoration of Jesus' crucifixion.

Literature

A study of contemporary literature also reveals a variety of images of Jesus. Walker Percy and Flannery O'Connor can be named among American authors for whom the image of Christ is an inspiration. Some contend that the Harry Potter books too contain 'inklings' of the Christian Gospel (see Connie Neal, *The Gospel according to Harry Potter*, London, Westminster: John Knox Press, 2002). Not everyone might agree with that, but the Christian theme is certainly to the fore in Tolkien's trilogy, *The Lord of the Rings*.

J.R.R. Tolkien and C.S. Lewis were colleagues in Oxford University. Both of them often discussed how best to express Christian faith in alternative shapes and forms without merely repeating Bible verses, or traditional creedal formulas. Their challenge was to create a new literature that would speak to traditional Christians as well as to readers who were alienated from Christianity. For Tolkien it was important that this literature would be a new, fresh forum in which the faith was implied rather than imposed, and suggested rather than preached.

What one does not find, therefore, in the *Rings* trilogy is explicit mention of 'Christ', but the reality of the Christian story is communicated throughout the text. The whole context of the events in Middle Earth speaks of a realm subject to a loving plan that, in Christian terms, would be referred to as Providence. Indeed the beautiful scenery speaks of a universe that is sacramental in that it seems to render visible something of the invisible light that envelopes the world and shines through.

The theme of the Ring is linked to the struggle between good and evil, a central theme also in the drama of Jesus' life, death and resurrection. Christian heroism, echoing Jesus' struggle, perseverance, and selflessness, seems to find expression, for example, in both Frodo and Sam. St Paul's words come to mind: 'It is when I am weak I am strong' (1 Cor 12:10). It could be said that the image of Jesus portrayed implicitly throughout the *Rings* is that of the defeated victor. Followers of this Jesus discover that neither strength nor intelligence is primary, but rather spiritual depth, being faithful to the end, adherence to the power of God and cultivation of faith, hope and charity, the virtues and Christ-attitudes that last.

Poetry
The Irish poet, Patrick Kavanagh, presents a sacramental image of Jesus present in the bits and pieces of life. What the poet wants to communicate is how very near Christ is to us. Kavanagh sees this presence of Jesus in relationships, circumstances and events. In other words, his image of Jesus is not a distant God beyond the stars in some far off sanctuary of the divine. The classic themes of incarnation and redemption are found in his writings as impacting on our everyday life.

> O Christ, that is what you have done for us:
> In a crumb of bread the whole mystery is.
> He read the symbol too sharply and turned
> From the five simple doors of sense
> To the door whose combination lock has puzzled
> Philosopher and priest and common dunce.
> Men build their heavens as they build their circles
> Of friends. God is in the bits and pieces of Everyday -
> A kiss here and a laugh again, and sometimes tears,
> A pearl necklace round the neck of poverty.
>   (from *Great Hunger*)

(See also Tom Stack's *No Earthly Estate: God and Patrick Kavanagh, An Anthology*, Dublin: Columba Press, 2002).

The Russian poet, Anna Akhmatova (1889-1966), while not as such a writer of religious poetry, comes across as a genuine believer and follower of Christ. Her first husband, Gumilev, was shot by the Soviets during the civil war circa 1920. Her son was imprisoned by Stalin for ten years as a way of keeping her under pressure. She persevered in writing magnificent poetry, much of which was only later published. Again her difficult life experience and her faith in the crucified Jesus Christ merged in poetic creativity and was expressed in works such as the short poem 'Crucifixion', itself part of a longer poem, 'Requiem'. The first part of 'Crucifixion' was written in Leningrad in 1940, the second part in Tashkent in 1943:

> **Crucifixion**
>
> 'Do not weep for me, Mother,
> I am in the grave.'
> 1
> A choir of angels sang the praises of that momentous hour,
> And the heavens dissolved in fire.
> To his Father He said: 'Why hast Thou forsaken me!'
> And to his Mother: 'Oh, do not weep for Me...'
> 2
> Mary Magdalen beat her breast and sobbed,
> The beloved disciple turned to stone.
> But where the silent Mother stood, there
> No one glanced and no one would have dared.

(In: *The Complete Poems of Anna Akhmatova*, translated by Judith Hemschemeyer, edited by Roberta Reeder, Edinburgh: Canongate Press, 1992, pp. 391-92).

Music

In the world of music we can point to musicians from various backgrounds that have clearly allowed Christian faith inspire their music: Arvo Paart (Estonia); Henryk Gorecki (Poland), James MacMillan (Scotland); John Tavener (England), and Olivier Messian (France).

Each artist who expresses his or her image of Jesus in art form has necessarily depicted a particular perspective. There is no one definitive image of Jesus. Each era has its particular focus or favourite.

The Church encourages artistic expression, recognising, however, that the greatest 'icon' of Jesus Christ has to be the very life of the Church community itself that has come down to us from the apostles who saw and heard Jesus first hand. The contemporary challenge for the Church is to enable people to 'see' Jesus and his founding vision through the way we live since Jesus himself told us: 'By this all will know you are my disciples, if you love one another'.

2

The Vision of Jesus in Context

Evidence for Jesus of Nazareth: religious sources
Jesus of Nazareth is a figure in history in the sense in which Alexander the Great or Julius Caesar, Joan of Arc or Marie-Therese of Austria, Charlemagne or Napoleon, Daniel O'Connell or Countess Markievicz are figures in history. He is not a character in history in the sense in which Cúchulainn or Fionn MacCumhaill or Pinocchio is a character. They are legends or myths, rich perhaps as types or heroes, but not real flesh and blood characters.

Jesus of Nazareth is not a myth or a legend. Neither is he a creation of the human imagination nor an invention of the first Christians. He was a flesh and blood character who lived in a small country called Palestine during the reigns of the first two Roman emperors, Augustus (as St Luke tells us in 2:1) and Tiberius (as Luke again informs us in 3:1).

Now this is of great importance, since the faith of Christian believers has always claimed that God became one of us and 'pitched his tent among us' so that his contemporaries, or some of them at any rate, 'saw his glory' (Jn 1:14). That faith believes that God *became and was* this Jesus from Nazareth. Jesus of Nazareth was therefore the ultimate message of God to humankind since he is God's very Son and infinite Word (Jn 1:1, 14).

Jesus was, besides, a light illuminating the mystery that surrounds our life. His words and deeds seemed to X-ray our human existence. Jesus is a kind of prism releasing the colours of our human nature. That was why St Paul called him 'the Last Adam' (I Cor 15:45): in him one finds the key to the mystery of every son and daughter of Adam.

God's very own Son became this Jesus (see Jn 1:14). God is unlimited, immortal, eternal and omnipotent. But in becoming this man, Jesus, whom the Gospels love to present as a shock to those who grew up with him (Lk 4:23-30), the Unlimited has joined himself to the limited, the Immortal has become mortal, the Eternal has intersected with time, and the Omnipotent is wrapped in swaddling clothes. 'Here', in the words of T.S. Eliot, 'the impossible union of spheres of existence is actual'.

This Jesus is therefore the focal point of history, as well as its goal. During the Liturgy of Holy Saturday night, as the priest puts the five grains of incense into the Paschal Candle, the five grains representing five wounds of the crucified Jesus of Nazareth, he says these words, 'Christ yesterday and today, the beginning and the end, the alpha and omega, all time belongs to him and all ages.'

The divine ocean in a human heart!
Here one encounters the good shock of Christianity, perhaps even the greatest shock, namely, that the total meaning of all reality and of all history coincides with this one historical individual. It is identical in fact with Jesus of Nazareth. He is the truth. He is the way, He is the life (Jn 14:6). No other individual in history has ever made any such claim.

This is the scandal of Christianity for the non-believer, while being its glory for believers who have bothered to reflect on the words of the creed they recite. It is the scandal of its positivity. 'The meaning of all beings is no longer to be found primarily in the sweep of mind which rises above the individual, the limited, into the universal... It is to be found in the midst of time, in the countenance of one man' (Joseph Ratzinger, *Introduction to Christianity*, New York, 1969, p. 141).

In more poetic words, Hans Urs von Balthasar, poet, historian and theologian, puts it like this: 'The divine Ocean forced into the tiny wellspring of a human Heart! The mighty oak-tree of divinity planted in the small, fragile pot of an earthly Heart! God, sublime on the throne of his majesty, and the Servant – toiling with sweat and kneeling with the dust of adoration – no longer to be distinguished from one another! ... All the treasures of God's wisdom and knowledge stored in the narrow chamber of human poverty! ...The rock of a divine certainty floating on the tides of an earthly hope!' (*Heart of the World*, San Francisco: Ignatius Press, 1979, p. 46).

Since Jesus is a figure in history – as well as the meaning of history, as believers claim – he can and should be approached 'historically'. Whoever would try to tell the story well should not neglect to vindicate, historically and critically, both Jesus Christ and Christian sources. This is an indispensable dimension of the teacher's task.

If Christianity claims to be founded on great and historical events and persons, uniquely on Jesus of Nazareth who became the Messiah and Lord (Acts 2:36), it is the responsibility of believers to be able to highlight the evidences for his historical existence. God became this human being! The essential content of our profession of faith is tied to the proclamation of the history of Jesus, the Son of God, who was born, died, and rose again for our salvation.

That this was what the very early, post-Pentecost Church did is clear from the *Acts of the Apostles*, which tells us what the very first Christians believed and did. We see there Peter's preaching. It consists in the main in the telling of the history of Jesus. A text or two will be enough to drive home the point:

> Men of Israel, hear these words: Jesus of Nazareth, a man attested to you by God with mighty works and

wonder and signs which God did through him in your midst, as you yourselves know – this Jesus, delivered up according to the definite plan and foreknowledge of God, you crucified and killed by the hands of lawless men. But God raised him up (2:22-4).

And in a second text, this time Peter is telling the story of Jesus to the household of the Roman officer, Cornelius:

> You must have heard about the recent happenings in Judaea; about Jesus of Nazareth and how he began in Galilee, after John had been preaching baptism. God had anointed him with the Holy Spirit and with power, and because God was with him, Jesus went about doing good and curing all who had fallen into the power of the devil. Now I, and those with me, can witness to everything he did throughout the countryside of Judaea and in Jerusalem itself: and also to the fact that they killed him by hanging him on a tree, yet three days afterwards God raised him to life and allowed him to be seen, not by the whole people but only by certain witnesses God had chosen beforehand. Now we are those witnesses (10: 37-41).

These two sample texts are enough to show that Christianity is eminently an historical religion since it is grounded on and rooted in great events and persons, uniquely in the person, life and death of Jesus of Nazareth. All this gives rise to the phenomenon of the New Testament that claims to complete the Old (see Lk 24:13-35). Still, we do not contemplate Christianity in written words, however special, nor in lifeless structures as if it were a mere museum religion, since its power is in the present, and its final revelation is of a new world that will come with the return in glory of the crucified and glorified Jesus at the end of history.

The questions arise: what are the sources for the existence and the 'life' of Jesus? Are they reliable? Do they allow us to access the historical Jesus of Nazareth, to discover his 'life'? These sources are religious (the Gospels and the New Testament letters of the Apostles) and secular (the Roman authors who mention Jesus, such as Pliny, Tacitus and Suetonius). We will look at these evidences in turn.

The historical reliability and the biographical nature of the Gospels
In the eighteenth century there began a heated debate as to the trustworthiness of the Gospels as history. The question posed was quite stark: are the Gospels more the products of the faith and belief of the early community than dependable accounts of the life, death and resurrection of Jesus of Nazareth? That was the question that was going to exercise theologians, historians and scholars right up to our times. Names such as Renan, Reimarus and Strauss are linked to the early years of this research.

Up to the eighteenth century the Gospels were seen as lives of Jesus, biographies. The new research, however, denied this description, and for a considerable length of time that was the state of play. In more recent times, the weight of scholarship has turned back to the original appellation of 'biographies', *but of a certain kind*. The reason for this about-turn is fascinating. Basically, the new research shows a very close connection between the Gospels and the format of ancient Greek and Roman biography. The Gospels are lives of Jesus, *but in this ancient sense*, not as in modern autobiographical novels.

As in the case of all sound research, the most recent scholars gather up the findings of their forerunners. Richard A. Burridge, an American scholar, shows that the majority of New Testament experts see the Gospels as genuine biographies. To show this Burridge takes ten lives of ancient Greek and Roman heroes and studies them (*Four Gospels, One Jesus?* Grand Rapids: Eerdmans, 1995).

What comes across from his research is that these *Lives* were not understood as some kind of video-taping or a recording of events moment by moment. Now when one realises that the Gospels are lives *in the sense that was normative and typical in the Greco-Roman milieu,* certain things become obvious and exciting.

While the chief characteristic of the biographical genre is indeed its exclusive attention to the subject, nevertheless, as the theological-Historical Commission for the Great Jubilee points out 'the tradition is very supple; sometimes a work will cover the entire life of the hero, sometimes only a period of it; sometimes it concentrates on the facts and on chronology, sometimes on certain themes, teachings, or virtues, without proceeding in chronological order' (*Jesus Christ, Word of the Father and Saviour of the World*, Rome, 1997, p. 60).

The biographical character of the Gospels

Burridge applies to the Gospels the same analysis used in dealing with the ten ancient Greek and Roman biographies, and he discovers remarkable parallels and similarities. The Gospels emerge as typical 'lives' in the sense current at the time.

First, concerning the *introductory notes*, Burridge emphasises that Matthew begins with the genealogy of Jesus, a characteristic element of the *bios* genre. Similarly, the prologue of Luke (1:1-4) is an actual historiographical introduction similar to the prologues of the biographical literature of the time (see also Feargus Ó Fearghail, 'The Literary Forms of Lk 1:5-25 and 1:26-38', *Marianum* [Rome], xliii (1981), pp. 321-344). In the second place, the subject of the Gospels is Jesus alone: the other characters revolve around him. Moreover, the Gospels concentrate on the last three years of Jesus' life, with a large portion dedicated to the last four days from Jesus' capture until the resurrection. This, too, squares with the research of Burridge into the ten ancient biographies where the first thirty or forty years are treated either very briefly or even omitted.

And everything that is said about the Synoptics, Matthew, Mark and Luke, may also be said about the Gospel of John.

John is thought to be less interested in what Jesus did than in making theological statements. A third of the Gospel is dedicated to Jesus' final week, his farewell, and his passion and death. This is not foreign to the genre. We can see this when we compare the Gospel of John with, for example, the Xenophon's Greek Tragedy, *Agesilaos*, in which thirty-seven per-cent of the narrative deals with the Persian campaign.

The Gospels, therefore, are genuine 'lives' of Jesus, answering to the typical genre of the time. They are not only the experience of the first Christian communities and the history of these communities. The *Acts of the Apostles* and the *Letters of St Paul* and the *Book of Revelation* can be said to be principally the experience of the primitive communities. The Gospels, however, are focused on the person of Jesus, his words and deeds, his ministry and, above all, his death on the cross and resurrection.

The formation of the Gospels

It is important to recall at this stage just how the Gospels came to be written. As we have seen, they are not the result of somebody sitting at a desk, writing up every evening the equivalent of a newspaper report on Jesus. In fact, there were three phases of the formation of the Gospels.

The first phase in the writing of the Gospels goes right back to Jesus' earthly existence on earth (his historical existence). Jesus spoke many words and performed many deeds. His three years of public ministry laid the foundation of the new movement of people that surrounded him, attracted by his words and deeds, converted by their encounter with him. All of these words and deeds, seen and heard, witnessed and experienced by many were to be the basis upon which the Gospels would eventually be written.

The second phase in the compilation of the Gospels began with the Apostolic preaching ('*kerygma*' in Greek). In the light of Jesus' death and resurrection, the Apostles went out with renewed courage and light to proclaim Jesus as risen from the dead. In their preaching, teaching, encouraging, they told about Jesus from their first-hand experience and witness. They had been with him, seen him, heard him, touched him (1 Jn 1:1-3). In the light of the Holy Spirit that came upon them at Pentecost, they now understood everything so much more clearly. They remembered episodes where things weren't so clear (e.g. Jesus talking about being the Temple that would be destroyed and rebuilt in three days) and now understood them in a much deeper way. So they transmitted memories, sayings, and stories to the community. As they communicated, they also understood anew. And all of this was guided by the Holy Spirit sent by the Risen Christ at this foundational moment in the life of the Church. This period of the Apostolic Preaching lasted about thirty years before a Gospel was written down!

The third phase came in the actual writing down of the Gospels (See Lk 4:1-4). Each of the Evangelists had a wealth of material to choose from, and each of the Evangelists wrote his Gospel, keeping an eye on the community to whom it was addressed. For instance, Matthew wrote to a more Jewish-centred community and so his Gospel reflects that dimension of Jesus' life and mission. Luke is writing to a more Gentile (non-Jewish) community and so his Gospel reflects that. This also explains why episodes may differ slightly. The writers of the Gospels are human authors who are divinely inspired. What they write is true because each episode of Jesus' life contains an infinity of meaning.

From the beginning the Gospels of Matthew, Mark, Luke and John were considered inspired. Others too wrote accounts of Jesus' life but they were not viewed as authoritative. What mattered most was that the Gospels of Matthew, Mark, Luke and John were linked directly or indirectly to the apostles, their accounts were based on the evidence of first-hand witnesses, and these Gospels were read when Christians met for worship.

The secular sources of evidence for Jesus of Nazareth

A great recent scholar has claimed that 'at no time was any [Roman] emperor free from anxiety about the 'Christian question' (C. H. Dodd, *The Founder of Christianity*, London 1971, p. 15). This was the question posed to the Roman Empire by the emergence of the Church of the first believers. We have already mentioned the first of the Emperors, Augustus (29 BCE-14 CE), who is mentioned by Luke in the latter's account of the nativity of Jesus (Lk 2:1), and the second, Tiberius, who was emperor during the public ministry of Jesus and his death and resurrection (14-37 CE) and is also mentioned by Luke (3:1). There are three Roman writers who explicitly mention the 'Christian question' in the second century. They are Pliny the Younger, Tacitus and Suetonius.

Pliny

The governor of the Roman province of Bithynia in Asia Minor, Pliny the Younger wrote a famous letter in 112 CE to the Emperor Trajan about some of his problems. He asked advice as to how to deal with people called 'Christians' whom he found in the province in great numbers. Through his informants he learned that they were a clandestine society. He arrested a number of these Christians and brought them to trial. The resulting examination found no evidence of crimes. At worst, they were the dupes of a 'degraded and extravagant superstition.' However, they refused to offer sacrifices to the emperor, being people of 'inflexible obstinacy' for which they deserved punishment. Pliny did discover, however, some of their practices consisting in 'meeting before dawn on an appointed day, and saying with one another a *form of words to Christ, as if to a god.*' One does not need to stretch the imagination to realise that this is the Eucharist. Pliny denounced the 'superstition' as a 'contagion spreading through villages and country, till the temples were emptied of worshippers.'

Tacitus

A friend of Pliny's, Tacitus was engaged in writing the history of the Rome of the Emperors, the famous *Annals*. He came to the reign of Nero (54-68 CE) and the Great Fire of 64 CE in his work. Rumour got around that the Emperor had started it and famously played the violin as the City burned. A scapegoat was needed. One was found in a body of people known as 'Christians.' They were so cruelly tortured that an initial public dislike began to turn to sympathy. His text is most informative, 'The author of that profession was *Christ, who, in the reign of Tiberius, was capitally punished by the procurator, Pontius Pilate. The deadly superstition* (sic!), though checked for a while, broke out afresh; and that, not only throughout Judaea, the original seat of the evil, but through the City... a vast multitude were convicted, not so much of firing the City, as of hatred of mankind' (*Annals*, XV, 44). Here we have an account from the hand of an informed author of the beginnings of Christianity in the execution of Jesus under the Roman Governor of Judaea.

Suetonius

Suetonius corroborates the testimony of Tacitus in these words, 'Capital punishments were inflicted on the Christians, a class of men of a *new and magical superstition.*' The famous English nineteenth-century scholar, writer and Cardinal, John Henry Newman, remarks that the context of this decree lends it particular significance, namely, it was one of various police regulations handed down by Nero (John Henry Newman, *An Essay on the Development of Christian Doctrine*, London, 1900, p. 209).

When seen together, these three Roman witnesses combine to provide the strongest possible evidence for the existence of Jesus Christ, and his followers. The 'Christians' are numerous in Rome already in the sixties of the first century and throughout the Provinces of the Empire by the beginning of the second century. And all this happened in spite of the fact that their founder had been executed as a criminal on the command of the Roman Governor in Judea, while his followers now sang to him as to a god!

The three Latin writers are unsympathetic in tone, but still informative of the facts. No doubt they would have been shocked had they returned to the great City a hundred or even fifty years later and seen the far greater spread of the 'deadly superstition', not only there but throughout the great Empire.

The impact of Rome

The Old Testament people chosen by God were given various titles such as 'people of Israel', 'children of Israel', 'sons and daughters of Abraham'. Their history is recounted in the pages of the Old Testament. This history was recognised as the history of God's interventions, not only on their behalf, but also on behalf of the whole of humankind. The Book of Jonah tells us as much.

Again John Henry Newman elegantly remarks, 'this is a history supernatural and almost scenic – it tells us what God is by telling us what he has done' (*Discussions and Arguments*, London, 1872, p. 294). The divinely-guided flow of that history was destined, in God's providence, to meet the expanding Republic of Rome and eventually the Roman Empire. But first it is important to look at how the way to the Roman presence was prepared.

Between the years 336 and 323 Alexander the Great, son of Philip of Macedon, conquered the whole known world of the time, reaching as far as India. The title 'the Great' seems altogether appropriate. In 333 he conquered Syria, then Tyre and Gaza and Egypt in rapid succession, founding his city, Alexandria, in 331 at the mouth of the Nile. He conquered the Persians whose empire had threatened for centuries to eclipse the Greeks. His victory brought with it a huge diffusion of Greek language and culture in the world of the time. This development has been called *Hellenization* (from *Hellas*, the Greek word for Greece).

Palestine, the land of the Jewish People, lay within this flow of influence. It is significant that the Jewish people living in Alexandria should want to translate their 'Writings' (Scriptures of the Old Testament) into Greek in the middle of the next century: according to legend, this was done by seventy learned Jews. The translation is known as the *Septuagint* (the Latin word for seventy).

At the beginning of the second century BCE, Antiochus Epiphanes initiated a persecution of the Jews. He pillaged the sacred Temple in Jerusalem in 170 BCE (1 Maccabees 1; 16f: II Mac 5:15f: Daniel 11:24-8). After a great massacre of Jews in 167, he decreed the abolition of all Jewish practices and established the cult of the Olympian Zeus in the Temple (I Macc 1:44f; II Macc 6:1f; Dn 11:31). This was the signal for revolt. Judas Maccabaeus led the revolt that lasted from 166 until 160 BCE.

Though the outcome was unsuccessful, the revolt had the effect of forging the national consciousness of the Jews who, now more than ever, connected faith and fatherland, religion and kingship. The religion of Israel, to be sure, was God's religion, given by God and authorised by him through patriarch and prophet. Its central religious features were God-given. However, the history of that people profoundly marked the gifts of God.

The religious and revealed categories forged throughout the course of Israel's almost bi-millennial history, such as Messiah, Priest, Covenant, Kingdom, to name but a few, were deeply rooted in Israelite history. God had indeed spoken through the 'scenic history' of the children of Israel. It is no surprise therefore if his great Words, such as those just mentioned, are coloured by the vicissitudes of that very history.

In 63 BCE the Romans under Pompey conquered Palestine and the surrounding area. Roman rule brought a degree of order and stability, and most of the peoples were reasonably happy to have it so. Perhaps the Jews were the exception to the rule. The Romans never quite understood the Jews who 'did not forget their brief spell of glory, and indulged a dangerous nostalgia' (C. H. Dodd, p. 18).

Reluctantly the Romans abandoned the idea of 'direct rule'. Instead, they organised the southern part of the country into the Roman province of Judaea, where less than two centuries later the Roman historian Tacitus saw all the trouble of the 'Christian question' beginning. First, the Romans appointed prefects to rule the province and later procurators. The capital was at Caesarea. Between 26 and 36 CE the Roman procurator was a man called Pontius Pilate.

The northern part of Palestine, known as Galilee, was put under a native prince, Herod Antipater I. Here begins the Herodian Dynasty whose members feature so frequently in the New Testament. Galilee was a real hot-bed of Jewish disaffection. This meant that the Roman Procurator had to keep a close eye on the thousands of Galileans who descended on Jerusalem annually for the celebration of the Passover. He transferred to Jerusalem from Caesarea for the duration and stationed a large number of troops in a castle overlooking the Temple courts.

Between Judaea and Galilee lay the region of Samaria. The Samaritans were a people of mixed race. Claiming even more loyalty to Moses and the Law than the Jews, they were despised by both Judaeans and Galileans as aliens and heretics. They did not accept the Temple in Jerusalem and had their own priesthood. In 35 CE Pontius Pilate ordered their massacre at Gerizim.

The socio-religious situation at the time of Jesus
As we have mentioned above, historical and political events left their mark on the socio-religious environment in which Jesus grew up and began his public ministry. At the time of Jesus

there existed, in fact, a number of religious groupings, each one with a distinctive view of how best to prepare for the Day of the Lord. Presumably Jesus would have had to consider which of them attracted him, which of them most corresponded to his own vision and mission.

The *Pharisees* were the most influential group. They arose after the Hellenistic reform period. Their scrupulous observance of the Law was an attempt at extending the sacredness of the Temple to everyday life. Motivated by a zeal for Judaism, the Pharisees developed a detailed programme of life – Sabbath observance, dietary laws and tithing – that helped Jews preserve their distinctiveness no matter where they went or what their walk of life was. In time a whole body of Pharisaic teaching developed parallel to biblical law.

The *Sadduccees* were a priestly class centred in the Temple of Jerusalem. They were more aristocratic. In terms of belief, they denied the afterlife.

The *Essenes* were people who formed a community that was highly apocalyptic in its thinking and practice. They felt it was necessary to flee from society because they believed the religious authorities had compromised with the Romans. They set up a community based on an imminent establishment of the Kingdom of God. This community followed a rigorous code of ethics and life-style. In the 1940s there was great excitement at the discovery of documents of the Essene community found in the Qumrân caves in the Holy Land.

The *Zealots* interpreted the coming of the Kingdom of God in political terms. For them armed revolt was essential in order to combat the unjust oppressors. They sought to re-establish the Davidic monarchy by force.

The *Baptisers* were those who were baptising people in the waters of the River Jordan. To be baptised was a sign of conversion as you awaited the 'day of the Lord'. From the Gospels, we know particularly of John the Baptist (Mk 1:1-8; Mt 3:1-6, 11-12; Lk 3:1-6, 15-18; Jn 1:19-34). He was preaching the need for conversion and penance before establishment of the kingdom of God.

What is significant is that out of all the groups, Jesus inserted himself into John the Baptist's penitential movement. In what might be called a messianic choice, Jesus chose the way of solidarity with those who felt the need for conversion and preparation for the coming of God's Kingdom.

Jesus immersed himself in the waters, allowing himself be baptised, a sign of his desire to share in our common destiny. He made himself one with us, one of us. Ultimately, it could be said that Jesus saw his life as one radical 'baptism', an immersion into the human condition that culminated on the cross. In Luke's Gospel, for instance, we hear Jesus say: 'I have a baptism with which to be baptized, and what stress I am under until it is completed' (12:50). Jesus follows the way of the 'Servant of the Lord' that we hear about in the Old Testament Book of Isaiah (chs 40-55).

The teachings of Jesus and their impact on the community: the Kingdom of God

Of great people it is often said that they lived by the message they proclaimed. One can readily think of good instances of such consistency between speaking and doing: an Oscar Romero, an Edel Quinn, a Mahatma Gandhi are a few that come instantly to mind.

Our age in fact requires this consistency, this follow-through, between word and deed. That is why it is has been said that modern men and women listen more willingly to witnesses than to teachers, and if they listen to teachers, it is because these are witnesses. The great attraction of our times is still the saint, like a Mother Teresa, and the hero, like a Gordon Wilson, and the martyr, like a Maximilian Kolbe.

This link between word and deed, the message and the action, stood out in the public life and activity of Jesus. The

Gospels love to speak of the authority of Jesus precisely in these terms. 'The peoples were amazed at his teaching, because he taught them as one who had authority, not as the teachers of the law' (Mk 1: 22).

St Luke tells us that 'Jesus began to do and to teach' (Acts 1:1). Jesus first lived what he taught and only then asked others to live it. In him truth and life are one. It was this harmony that attracted the crowds and it was this same harmony that was the secret of the deep impression that his presence made upon the men and women, young and old, whom he met along the roads and in the towns of first-century Palestine.

Jesus' teaching was not separable from his person. It is in fact the clue to his identity as the Son of God made man and living among his creatures, on whom he sheds the light of his glory (see Jn 1:14; 2:11; 2Cor 4:6).

What did he teach? What was his message as embodied in the dynamic link between his person, his words and his deeds? The first three Gospels are unanimous in stating that the vivifying centre of his whole life was the Kingdom of God. In fact St Mark's Gospel, which opens with an excitement of narration like that of an athlete telling his peers the thoughts careering through his mind during the last laps of that victorious final, begins abruptly,

'After John had been arrested, Jesus went into Galilee. There he proclaimed the good news from God. "The time has come", he said, "and the Kingdom of God is close at hand. Repent, and believe the Good News"' (Mk 1:14-15).

It is enough to begin to study Jesus and his ministry in order to encounter his preoccupation with the Kingdom of God. But what is the Kingdom of God? It is difficult to render the term in a comparable English phrase, but the main point is that the Kingdom of God is not something limited to a physical space, nor is it bound to a system of truths and commandments.

For the past hundred years or so the translation, 'rule of God', has come to the fore. The Kingdom of God, then, would be where God rules. God is King because he rules. This sounds fine and dynamic, but on reflection it may not be so dynamic at all! For many people, both in the past and today, suffer under many kinds of seizures of power in professional, political and personal life. This fact should perhaps caution us against the use of this translation. 'We should like to know first how God rules' (Jürgen Moltmann, *Jesus Christ for Today's World*, London, 1994, p. 8).

Fortunately, we can see how God rules in the person, the deeds and the words of Jesus; since Jesus himself is the Kingdom of God, as the Fathers of the Church loved to stress. 'The Kingdom of God is thus the hidden but powerful presence of God in Jesus restoring wholeness and life' to humanity. And yet a great paradox becomes evident at once in that 'the greatest resistance to Jesus was provoked by the fact that God's power at work in him showed itself as a power of incomprehensible love' (R. Kerestzy, *Jesus Christ. Fundamentals of Christology*, New York, 1991, p.84).

The kind of God Jesus manifests is too good to be true! All this demands that we look seriously at the Kingdom of God as it emerges in the person and teaching of Jesus.

Jürgen Moltmann suggests an excellent method to discover the full meaning of the reality involved. He follows the principle that 'it is one thing to learn the concept of happiness, and another to be happy. And so it is one thing to reduce the kingdom of God to a definition, and another to experience it, to feel it, to see it and to taste it. It is not the term that must be allowed to define the experience. Rather, the experience must define the term'. In the light of this principle Moltmann proposes a threefold approach following the method, 'see-judge-act' (J. Moltmann, p. 9f).

To 'see' the Kingdom of God it is enough to look carefully at the public ministry of Jesus of Nazareth, for his public life is an epiphany of the Kingdom. To 'judge' or understand the Kingdom it is enough to formulate the correct questions regarding what Jesus actually meant and conveyed. Finally, to 'act' is to translate into my everyday living the principles of the Kingdom so that the Kingdom enters me and I enter into the Kingdom. We will now look at these stages ('see', 'judge' and 'act') in turn.

See the Kingdom: four biblical Perspectives

(i) *The Kingdom of God in parables*
In his teaching Jesus talks about the Kingdom of God in comparisons or parables that he takes from the world of nature and the world of human beings. Perhaps a really good example of this teaching is to be found in chapter four of St Mark's Gospel. There one finds a sequence of parables drawn from the world of nature: the parables of the sower and the seed, and the parable of the mustard seed.

The sower going out to sow scatters generously the seed in the hope that each grain will germinate in the soil, flourish in the summer and bear fruit in abundance. This is like the Kingdom of God: the seed is the Word of God and it is sown in our lives. Both time and our generous response constitute the soil, the good soil, where it can germinate and yield a harvest.

In Luke chapter 15 we have another group of parables. These are the lost and found parables – the lost sheep, the lost son, and the lost coin. There is more joy in heaven over one sinner who repents than over ninety-nine just and upright people who do not have to repent. In the parable of the lost son, the joy of the Father is so great that he says, 'This my son was dead, and is alive again; he was lost and is found' (15:24).

What, then, is the Kingdom according to these parables? 'It is nothing other than God's joy at finding again the beings he created who have been lost. And what is the "repentance" that the sinner has to perform? It is nothing other than the being-found, and the return home from exile and estrangement, the coming-alive again, and the joining in God's joy' (J. Moltmann, p. 12).

Luke chapter 15 opens with a rather dramatic setting for these parables, which, pagoda-like, build one on top of the other to reinforce one and the same message, '"This man", the scribes and the Pharisees complained, "welcomes sinners and eats with them"' (15:3). In the minds of the scribes and the Pharisees, two sections of Israelite society, God could have no interest in those far from him, those who were sinners. But Jesus showed the opposite to be the actual case: God is a Father and has only one thing in his heart, namely, the good of all his children, for now and for ever. And so he is prodigal in his mercy and goodness and love (See John Paul II's encyclical, *Dives in Misericordia*, 1980, chapter IV 5-6).

(ii) The Kingdom of God in the healing of the sick
The first thing that people discovered about Jesus was the healing power of the divine Spirit. His very person and presence are depicted in the Gospels as magnets that draw people out of the shadows and corners into which they have been pushed. 'That evening at sundown, they brought to him all those who were sick or possessed with demons. And the whole city was gathered together about the door. And he healed many who were sick with various diseases, and cast out many demons' (Mk 1:32f). Now while miraculous healings were common in the Old Testament, those performed by Jesus have a very particular context. They are part of the coming of God's kingdom. In the elegant words of Moltmann, 'The kingdom of the living God drives out the germs of death and spreads the seeds of life'.

(iii) The Kingdom of God in the companionship of Jesus
What is so striking in the Gospels is the fact that Jesus seeks out the 'sinners and the tax-collectors'. He demonstrated this publicly through his table-fellowship with them. The

respectable people complain, as we have seen, that 'this man receives sinners and eats with them' (Lk 15:2).

When Jesus is at the banquet thrown by the recently converted tax-collector, Matthew, he explains his attitude with exceptional power, 'It is not the healthy who need the doctor but the sick. "Go and learn the meaning of the words: What I want is mercy, not sacrifice" (Hosea 6:6). And indeed I did not come to call the virtuous, but sinners' (9:12-3). How extraordinary! Jesus begins with a proverb, then quotes the Scriptures, and finally states the policy underpinning his own practice.

The Kingdom comes in the form of mercy which is embodied in Jesus and which radiates on those he meets, especially the most abandoned. As radium penetrates to diseased cells in the body restoring health and wholeness, so does the merciful love of Jesus of Nazareth penetrate to the deepest recesses of the heart in order to heal and renew. Jesus is truly a doctor.

Mercy, in fact, is what happens when God's goodness meets human misery, and what misery is greater than that of being far away from him who is the source of all life and love? In this process Jesus wished to save both the good and the unjust. The former are frequently tempted to judge others negatively, seeing the speck of sawdust in the brother's eye and paying no attention to the plank in their own eye (Mt 7:3). In that way they are tempted to self-righteousness and hardness of heart. If undetected and uncorrected, this can close them to the Kingdom that Jesus is setting up for all, sinners and just together.

(iv) The Kingdom of God in the poor, the children and the women

The quality of Jesus' presence among and to people is unique. This quality transforms minds and hearts bringing the sick, the sinners and the lost into the Kingdom. The same dynamic logic pushes Jesus towards the most defenceless in society, the people who socially and legally are non-persons. The measure of their vulnerability becomes the measure of Jesus' generosity.

The poor not only have nothing, they are nothing on the scales of this world. 'The collective term "the poor" embraces the hungry, the unemployed, the enslaved, the people who have lost heart and lost hope, and the suffering' (J. Moltmann, p. 17). For all of these, Jesus of Nazareth was good news.

It is legitimate perhaps to single out a few categories for specific mention. There are the poor as just defined, women and children. What Jesus brings to the poor is not primarily the aid of charitable works but the realisation of their true dignity as children of the One he called 'Abba, Father'. In that way they could discover their indestructible worth in the eyes of the Creator.

And not only that, but they find the energy to rise up out of their destitution, material and human, and to bring peace to the violence of the inhumanity and the injustice that enslaved them in the first instance. It is in that way that they rise and take the Kingdom of God by force, and it is in that way that the Kingdom belongs to them (Mt 5:3).

Jesus' attitude to women is remarkably new. The gospel of Jesus' words and deeds is a strong protest against oppressive attitudes, and a clear affirmation of women's inalienable dignity. He does not discriminate against foreign women (he heals the daughter of the Syro-Phoenician woman: Mk 7:24-30). He overcomes the taboo concerning their impurity under the law (he heals the woman diseased with an issue of blood: Mk 5:34). He indicates women as an example (he lauds the poor widow: Mk 12:41-4) and cultivates their friendship (he is a close friend of Martha and Mary, the sisters of Lazarus: Lk 10:38-42; Jn 11).

In recent years, there has been a discovery of the significance of what the Gospel tells us about women. One contemporary scholar, Elisabeth Moltmann-Wendel, has written that 'the Bible has within its pages a unique history of the greatness, the sovereignty, the wisdom and the courage of women. It is perhaps the most interesting book in connection with the emancipation of women' (*The Women around Jesus*, London: SCM, 1982, p. 6).

A particularly poignant instance of Jesus' liberating attitude towards the women he met is to be seen in his dialogue with the Samaritan woman (Jn 4). This woman is, in the eyes of men, even good men, inferior to them by the very fact of being a woman, while to her Jewish neighbours she is a heretic, and to her fellow-villagers an adulteress. And yet Jesus' dialogue with her is his longest dialogue with any individual person recorded in the Gospels. On that score Jesus transcended the culture of his times and the prejudices of his contemporaries.

The truth is that the motive for his revolutionary action lay in the truth of our creation 'in the image and the likeness of God' (Gen 1:27). He had come to reclaim this dignity by the gospel of his person, deeds and words, and especially by his passion, death and resurrection, so that in Jesus 'there is neither Jew nor Greek, slave nor free, male nor female' (Gal 3:28).

Jesus destroys the many forms of religious and cultural apartheid that set persons and groupings of persons in opposition to one another and to his Father's design. 'May they all be one' (Jn 17:21) is not only the prayer summing up his whole life mission, it is also as Pope John Paul puts it 'the deepest desire of Jesus' heart'.

Finally, there were the children. At the time of Jesus a child was a defective adult. Fondness for them would be just as unintelligible as preference for the acorn over the oak tree. When the disciples turn them away Jesus declares, 'Let the little children alone, and do not stop them coming to me; for it is to such as these that the kingdom of heaven belongs' (Mt 19:14; see Mk 10:13-6; Lk 18:15-17). He even goes further: the child is nominated as the norm for all others. Clearly this is not a glorification of infantilism or of childishness. Rather, it is the declaration that in the Kingdom there is but one Father of many children, and we are the many children of that same Father (Mt 23; Acts 17:28). The naturalness and the trust of the child best embody the indispensable dispositions for entry into the Kingdom. 'Truly, I say to you, unless you turn and become like children, you will never enter the Kingdom of heaven' (Mt 18:3).

The great German theologian, Karl Rahner, has written: 'Childhood is openness, the courage to allow fresh horizons, ever new and ever wider, to be opened up before one, a readiness to journey into the untried and the untested' (K. Rahner, 'Towards a Theology of Childhood', in *Theological Investigations*, vol. 8, London and New York, 1971, p. 48).

This is why the most recent doctor of the Church (there are only thirty-three such people in the history of the Church!), Thérèse of Lisieux, never wanted to be an adult in the normal meaning of the word. 'The one who brought the Kingdom of God close to us brings the poor and the children close to us too. They are his family, his people, for they too represent God's kingdom in this world of violence' (see J. Moltmann, p. 19).

Judge and understand the Kingdom: some theological clarifications

The foregoing perspectives provide some understanding of the Kingdom of God as the focus of the public ministry of Jesus. Inevitably, certain theological questions arise from these very same insights. We will consider very briefly the principal questions.

(i) Is the Kingdom of God present or future?
In the light of what we have just said, the answer is not difficult. The Kingdom of God is experienced in the present in the companionship of Jesus! It is experienced where those lost in evil and in aimlessness of purpose are found, where the unjust are changed to care for the weak, where the poor have their dignity recognised and restored, where women and children are treated according to the truth of their status as children of the one Father, there the Kingdom of God begins.

The Kingdom begins there as a seed which acorn-like grows to become the tree in which the birds of the air build their nests. The Kingdom is therefore also an object of hope, albeit a hope rooted in experience and in memory. In that way the Kingdom involves the tension between something that exists already and still has to mature into fullness and completion. That is why Jesus teaches us to pray, 'Our Father, thy Kingdom come!' (Lk 11:2).

(ii) Does the Kingdom of God belong to this world or the next?
No doubt some people who see the Kingdom as belonging to the next world will quickly quote the answer of Jesus to Pilate, 'My kingdom is not of this world' (Jn 18:36). Moltmann perceptively points out, however, that this is not a statement about the place of the kingdom but about its origin (Moltmann, p. 20).

The truth is that the Kingdom is 'in' this world but not 'of' this world. It is not any kind of outgrowth of this world, but a gift from the Creator of this world from whom every good gift descends (Jn 1:17). And it is precisely in the person of Jesus who has come into this world of flesh and blood that it has been enfleshed. However, it encompasses both heaven and earth. That is why Jesus teaches us in the prayer of all prayers that we are to ask that the Kingdom will come 'on earth as it is in heaven'.

(iii)Is the Kingdom of God exclusively the affair of God or are we also involved?

In answering this question one touches upon the currents of thought and action that have determined much of the history of recent centuries. The renowned philosopher and theologian, Eric Voegelin, has shown decisively that the great ideologies of recent centuries all derived from a single aspiration – the desire to bring the kingdom of God on earth entirely but as a purely human achievement (Eric Voegelin, *The New Science of Politics*, Chicago, 1952).

This would remove the dramatic tension between divine operation and human co-operation, since there would have to be only one principal actor, the great Ideologue-Leader himself, be he a Comte, a Marx, a Freud or a Nietzsche and his Superman. Inevitably God would become superfluous since replaced by a this-worldly leader capable of inaugurating the earthly kingdom of God. Besides, the Christian message of the Kingdom, it was claimed, tends to alienate Christians from serious involvement in the project of building the earthly city. It does this as a result of its insistence upon the life that is to come.

That this can happen *to some Christians* is no doubt possible. History is evidence of the fact. John Henry Newman has described the danger in these terms, 'When persons are convinced that life is short... when they feel that the next life is all in all, and that eternity is the only subject that really can claim or fill their thoughts, then they are apt to undervalue this life altogether, and to forget its real importance. They are apt to wish to spend the time of their sojourning here in a positive separation from active and social duties: yet it should be recollected that the employments of this world though not themselves heavenly, are, after all the way to heaven... but it is difficult to realize this. It is difficult to realize both truths at once, and to connect both truths together; steadily to contemplate the life to come, yet to act in this' (John Henry Newman, *Parochial and Plain Sermons*, VIII, London, 1878, pp. 154-5).

And it is the fact of some Christians being so heavenly minded that they are of no earthly good that may be responsible for thinkers like Nietzsche concluding that the Christian is a useless, separated, resigned person, extraneous to the progress of the world.

This great issue, as Newman saw, is a difficult one. It is difficult since it requires us neither to think in dualistic terms, nor in either/or terms. Fortunately, it was magisterially addressed in the Second Vatican Council. The Pastoral Constitution on the Church in the Modern World, states categorically, 'The Christian message, far from deterring us from the task of building up the world... binds us, rather, to all this by a still more stringent obligation' (*Gaudium et Spes*, 34, see also nn. 39). Still it is difficult for some people to realise the interpenetration of heaven and earth.

Once again it is Jesus' own person and teaching that vividly describes this interconnection. His teaching shows that God's kingdom is Jesus' affair, since he alone is capable of bringing it. This was, as we have seen earlier, the powerful experience of those who had the experience of Jesus! But Jesus makes it our responsibility too! That's why to the man who was willing to follow him without reservation if only he could first bury his father, Jesus says, 'Leave the dead to bury their dead; your duty is to go and spread the news of the Kingdom of God' (Lk 9:60).

(iv) Is the Kingdom of God a theocracy or is it union with the living God?

If one translates the term Kingdom of God as 'rule of God', there is an undeniable overtone of theocracy about the notion. However, in the light of our first descriptive section on the nature of the Kingdom, it is clear that the true notion excludes any suggestion of control.

Rather, the Kingdom is where true freedom is to be found precisely because it is the place where the insatiable human hunger for mystery, love, truth, beauty and freedom are perfectly realised. St Paul is quite explicit, 'The Kingdom of God is not a matter of eating and drinking, but of righteousness, peace and joy in the Holy Spirit' (Rom 14:17). The Kingdom of God is our home, indeed our lasting city (Heb 13:14).

When God ventures forth to us in his Son made flesh of our flesh then there is the fullest participation of the divine in the human, and there is the correlative possibility of the human to venture into the expansive space of the divine, so that the human participates in the divine.

That becomes a breathtaking adventure! And it is the adventure of the Christian who follows Jesus of Nazareth. It begins now or else it will not begin at all! However, it will come to fruition only in the restoration of all things when there will be 'a new heavens and a new earth' (Rev 21:1) and Jesus will hand over the Kingdom to the Father (I Cor 15:24).

Act now by making the unconditional choice of the Kingdom of God!

Jesus stresses the urgency with which the Kingdom is to be welcomed. This welcoming cannot brook any procrastination whatsoever. 'The Kingdom of God is at hand; repent and believe in the gospel' (Mk 1:15). The presence of the Kingdom is a gift and an imperative, or rather an imperative flowing from a gift.

The offer of this gift is urgent in the sense that, as a treasure unparalleled, it must be taken quickly or the opportunity may come no more. The time to enter the kingdom is now, in fact, this present moment. To postpone is to show that one's heart is attached to that which is not God, like the rich young man (Mk 10:17-22). It is also to miss the special time of the Lord's visitation (Mt 23:37-9).

What is time? It is a flow of before and after. We experience this fact in the phenomenon of the fleeting away of the hours, the days and the months. This experience drives home the lesson that time is not under our control and, worse still, that we are time-dominated and therefore radically temporal creatures.

The flow of time creates in us the sense of dispersion, of being scattered. And this realisation in turn makes us be on the look out for a focus, a centre, or a place that is not vulnerable to such scattering. We leave only vanishing footprints on the shifting sands of time. The great Latin poet, Horace (65 – 8 BCE) put it poignantly, *Immortalia ne speres, monet annus et alma quae rapit hora diem* (Both the year and the pleasant hour that snatches away the day advise: do not hope for immortal things).

The frequent reaction made to this experience is to construct our own future. We do so in order to achieve a measure of control over our vanishing time. This planning is both the driving force of our activity as well as the source of our daily anxiety. There is one thing, however, that that planning leaves completely out of the reckoning: there may be no future, and even if there is, it may not turn out at all as we had planned.

Now it is into this very human situation that Jesus comes and, impelled by the fire of the Kingdom, announces: God comes from the Beyond into the Here. He comes from the Eternal into the Now. Klaus Hemmerle, a German theologian puts it like this: 'The source of the future becomes present for us, God comes from the periphery of time into the centre of time' (*Glauben-wie geht das?*, Freiburg im Breisgau, 1978, p. 29). Jesus Christ is here and He is now! He is radically with us and He is radically for us. He wants to have his Time with us so that we can have all time with him, and so have His future, His absolute future as our very own future. However, the only Moment in which we can receive that future is now, where the Eternal intersects with Time.

There is only one option that is sane: to make God the centre of life, God and his kingdom. If up until now the Kingdom was at the periphery of life, it must become the centre. His Kingdom is the true focus of human existence. It is to become the ideal of one's life!

Is this asking too much from frail human beings? Not at all, since Faith asks us to sell our worries and to bury our fears, and, like the lilies in the fields and the birds of the air (Mt 7:26, 28-9), to live fully in the now of God, because his eternity has intersected with each and every moment of time, and that means my time too!

This carefree attitude is, in no way, an inactivity. On the contrary, it corresponds perfectly to the total determination one ought to have for such a gift as the Kingdom, which one must 'seek first and then everything else will be given as well', including 'father, mother, brothers, sisters and lands' (Mt 6:33; Mk 10:29-31). Then everything depends on us as well! A new beginning must take place!

And this explains the fact that the proclamation of the Kingdom, as recorded in Mark, is followed immediately by the calling of the first four disciples. This vocation to discipleship is not a demand, nor a claim but a logical and rational response to the gift of God. It is precisely this gift which is the 'good news', while the taking of this gift is faith and conversion. Faith, then, follows upon the proclamation of the Kingdom of God present in Jesus. For either God is all-important, or else he is not important at all!

The words of Elizabeth-Anne Steward provide an eloquent summary of what it means to see, judge and act in the light of the Kingdom of God preached and brought among us by Jesus: 'The new order to which Jesus pointed demands a transformation of consciousness, a completely new way of seeing which, in turn, necessitates new ways of thinking, new ways of being... To participate in the reign of God, then, means nothing less than undergoing "an interior revolution"... How threatening all this is, and yet, as Jesus pointed out, unless we undergo a complete transformation we will not make any progress, spiritually speaking... To allow oneself to be transformed is the first step towards renewing the earth' (*Jesus, the Holy Fool*, Franklin, Wisconsin: Sheed&Ward, 1999, p. 90).

3
The Message in Conflict

3.1 Conflict with Establishment

It is not easy to understand a recurring phenomenon in history: the frequency with which great men and women end their lives in violence at the hands of their contemporaries. Even more perplexing is the abiding fact of unsolicited murder of great and good people.

The martyrs, for instance, are a great stain on the human story, their deeds and witness standing there intrepidly in accusation of their killers, to whom they wished only good and no harm. The names of Gandhi, Oscar Romero, Joan of Arc and Socrates jump to mind. Somehow their killers missed the life and truth they embodied. Socrates' biographer and pupil, Plato (428 – 348 BCE), in his account, *The Trial of Socrates*, provides a classical statement on the abiding danger of missing authentic life.

How did it happen that Jesus had to endure a rising tide of hostility and eventually death on the wood of the cross, the ultimate degradation of which Roman society was capable? 'They hated me without reason,' (Jn 15:25) Jesus said at one moment in his ministry. Why? It is not easy to understand the hatred against the good. Such aversion is still a fact of life, a tragic monument in our history. It throws a sombre shadow across the human story.

In the light of the crucifixion of the Son of God, Paul, the ex-persecutor of the early followers of Jesus of Nazareth, could write, about twenty years after the event, 'The human race has nothing to boast about before God', for it 'crucified the Lord of glory.' (I Cor 1:29; 2:8). The crucified Christ, in Paul's vision of things, stood there as evidence of humanity's depravity, of our crime of deicide.

But how, concretely, did it come about that he who brought good news to the poor, sight to the blind, liberty to captives (Lk 4:18-21) should himself fall foul of those to whom he was sent? 'He came to his own people and they did not accept him.' (Jn 1:12). Why? Why did the very enemies of his own people, the Romans, make common cause with the leading members of the nation of Israel against the Holy One of God, who had come so that 'they might have life and have it to the full' (Jn 10:10)? For this is precisely what they did according to the first 'history' of the primitive Church (Acts 3:13-5).

To begin a response to the question 'why', we will need to examine the claims, actions and outreach of Jesus. It is important, however, to state at the outset that in reading the Gospel accounts of Jesus' interaction with his contemporaries we need to be careful not to rush to any generalisations about Jesus' death and the Jewish people.

In recent years within Christianity, it is recognised that much greater care is needed in talking about Jesus' relationship with the Jews. It must always be recalled that Jesus himself was a Jew, so were his apostles, his mother, his immediate followers. Jesus followed the Jewish traditions and practices.

The Gospels at no point say that all Jews were to blame for the death of Jesus. The issues here are complex and need very careful reading of Gospel texts. Ultimately, what comes across in the Gospels is that it is the sinfulness of humanity that led to Jesus' death. It was his confrontation with evil, which must be eradicated from all human hearts, that ultimately led to his death on the Cross (see the Congregation of the Faith document that can be accessed on the Vatican website: *The Jewish People and their Sacred Scriptures in the Church* (2001); see also Sarah Tanzer, 'Jewish-Christian Relations and the Gospel of John', *The Bible Today*, 40 (2002), pp. 99-105).

The claims of Jesus of Nazareth
In his teaching, Jesus did not speak and conduct himself like an ordinary rabbi, prophet or teacher of wisdom. Jesus' own contemporaries noticed the difference and asked with amazement, 'What is this? A new teaching and one proclaimed with authority' (Mk 1:27). Jesus went beyond the Law in the sense that he went above the Law.

There are some shining examples in the Sermon on the Mount. For example, 'You have learnt how it was said to our ancestors, You must not kill; and if anyone does kill he must answer for it before the court. But I say this to you: anyone who is angry with his brother will answer for it before the court' (Mt 5:21-2). There follow in quick succession five further such teachings.

Now what is important to notice here is that Jesus quotes Moses but only to correct him! 'He placed his word, not against, but above, the highest authority in Judaism, the word of Moses. And behind the authority of Moses was the authority of God.' (W. Kasper, *Jesus the Christ*, London, 1976, p. 102). Jesus claims to say God's last word, a word that brings the word of God in the Old Testament to its ultimate fulfilment.

Jesus also speaks in a different way from a prophet. The prophets use formulas such as 'The Word of the Lord came to me', or 'Thus says the Lord', or 'A saying of Yahweh'. Jesus, however, never speaks in this fashion. Instead, he makes no distinction between his word and God's! (Mk 1:22; 27; 2:10).

The only category that does justice to Jesus' behaviour and attitude is that he is *the Messiah*, who would not abolish the Law but interpret it in another way. Jesus regarded himself as God's mouth, as God's voice. And his contemporaries saw his claim that way and rejected it as blasphemy (Mk 2:7).

There is a third dimension in Jesus' behaviour that points in the same direction and that inevitably challenged those who encountered him. He linked the decision to accept the Kingdom of God specifically to the decision for or against himself, his word and his work. The link is particularly clear in Mt 10:32-3, 'Whoever acknowledges me before men, I will also acknowledge him before my Father in heaven. But whoever disowns me before men, I will disown him before my Father in heaven.' To choose Jesus is to enter the Kingdom of God. Once again one sees that Jesus is the Kingdom of God in person.

Jesus' call to discipleship also points to his authority as God's mouthpiece, his ultimate Word standing forth in the world. Jesus chose those 'whom he wanted' (Mk 3:13). They did not choose him. His choice is the catalyst in the whole affair. And his call, 'Follow me' (Mk 1:17), is not only a command but also 'a creative word that makes disciples of those to whom it is spoken' (Mk 1:17; 3:14). It is interesting that in the account of the call of the Twelve, Mark says that 'he made Twelve' (Mk 3:14). This re-creation of those whom he called means that they are 'to be with him' by sharing in his mission and destiny to bring the Kingdom of God. The choice of Jesus in respect of the person is meant to re-create the person.

When one puts together these claims of Jesus one is brought face to face with someone utterly unique. 'In Jesus we see God and his glory. In him we come into contact with God's grace and God's judgement. He is God's kingdom, God's word and God's love in person... And yet... he is poor and homeless. He is among his disciples like one who serves (Lk 22:27)' (Kasper, pp. 103-104). The mystery of his identity deepens, for his claims occur in a setting of rare humility (Mt 11:28-30), poverty (Lk 12:33) and gentleness (Mt 11:29).

The actions of Jesus

It was not only his teaching and attitude that caused offence to the Judaism of the day. His teaching was a shock, but his action was a revelation, indeed a revolution. His very lifestyle – in particular, his closeness to sinners, the suffering, those in the grip of evil, and those whose lives had been warped by any form of twisted religion (James 1:27) – sent waves of amazement through the society of the day.

As we have seen when looking at his bringing of the Kingdom of God, he befriended sinners of all kinds (Lk 5:29-32; 15:1-3). In the minds of the powerful categories in the society of the day, such as the Scribes and the Pharisees, this association brought about ritual uncleanness. He even set up table fellowship with them as a sign of God's unconditional welcome and a token of the mercy that could re-make their lives. In Jesus, people like the tax-collector, Zacchaeus (Lk 19:1-10), or the civil servant, Matthew (Mt 9:9-13) met with a life-changing and life-transforming mercy, for mercy is what happens whenever God's unconditional love encounters the human misery of sin (Lk 9:35-7).

The cost of this, however, was enormous for Jesus personally: he began to encounter first the suspicion and then the wrath of the Pharisees and the Sadduccees, to the point of being called a 'glutton and a drunkard, a friend of tax collectors and sinners' (Mt 11:19). He definitely could not be a prophet or the Messiah: in fact, he seemed worse than a sinner, because he was a blasphemer, and that in the eyes of the most prestigious echelons of Israelite society.

C.H. Dodd writes that 'The term [blasphemer] is a heavily loaded one, and the charge suggests an affront to the powerful sentiments of religious reverence and awe, evoking both hatred and fear. The charge of blasphemy expresses not so much a rational judgement as a passionate, almost instinctive, revulsion of feeling against what seems to be a violation of sanctities. There must have been something about the way he spoke and acted which provoked this kind of revulsion in minds conditioned by background, training and habit. It was this, over and above reasoned objections to certain features of his teaching, that drove the Pharisees into the unnatural (and strictly temporary) alliance with the worldly hierarchy, whose motives for pursuing Jesus to death were quite other' (C. H. Dodd, pp. 78-9).

A good instance of this animosity is to be seen in Mark 7 where these groups challenge him precisely for his cavalier attitude to the regulations added by the rabbis to the Mosaic Law, in this instance the washing of hands before eating. Here Jesus encounters the relegation of the Holy Law of the Holy God of the Old Covenant to a role subordinate to that of a rabbinical regulation. It is time to intervene. The exterior has taken over from the interior, the appearances are more important than the heart.

Jesus begins with their prophets, 'This people honours me with their lips, while their hearts are far from me' (Is 29:13). As if this was not bad enough, he even speaks of the destruction of the Temple, the very heartbeat of the holy religion of Israel (Jn 2:19).

The outreach of Jesus

There is a dimension of Jesus of Nazareth's outreach that is most striking: he reaches towards non-Jews, such as Romans, and towards heretics, such as Samaritans. There is the famous instance of the latter in the case of the Samaritan woman (Jn 4) to which we have already alluded. Her reaction to Jesus' request for a drink of water is sharp and tough, 'What? You are a Jew and you ask me, a Samaritan, for a drink? Jews, in fact, do not associate with Samaritans' (4:9). At the end of a fascinating dialogue/conversation Jesus even tells her directly his identity as the Messiah and then sends her into the town to announce him to her fellow-villagers. While 'salvation comes from the Jews' (4:22), it is for the whole world (4:42).

The Roman officer who requests Jesus' intervention to save the life of his little son suggests that there is no need for Jesus to come in person but merely to give the command. Jesus is so surprised at the Roman's faith that he praises the faith of the officer in words that would not gratify him to the religious authorities of the time, 'I tell you, I have not found such great faith even in Israel' (Lk 7:9).

Casting the fire of God on the earth
In all of the public ministry of Jesus, every aspect of which is dedicated to the inauguration of the Kingdom of God, one notices the fire that drove him in that ministry. 'I have come to bring fire on the earth, and how I wish it were already kindled' (Lk 12:49). What was that fire? It was the fire of God's undying love that had come into the world and that was identical with this Jesus of Nazareth. It was the fire of the good God of Creation whose zealous love longed to see the healing and full realisation of men and women created in his own image and likeness, but who had fallen into the prison of evil and the death of despair.

Now there stood forth in the world the emissary of this God, his own very Son become flesh of one of the children of Israel, Mary of Nazareth. He looked at the multitudes and, 'having compassion on the crowd' (Mt 15:32), said, 'You must not die'. To love someone, Gabriel Marcel tells us, is to say, 'You cannot die.' Jesus stared death in the eye and said, 'O death, I will be your death' (1 Cor 15:55).

In the elegant words of Jürgen Moltmann, 'The history of Christ is the history of a great passion, a passionate love. And just because of that, it became at the same time the history of a deadly agony' (Moltmann, p. 31). From beginning to end Jesus is pro-active. He is not the passive victim of the unfolding circumstances of his ministry. He wants to see lives changed, society remade, and history redirected according to the mysterious prototype of an eternal love that had appeared in space and in time, and walked in flesh and blood and with a human heart on the roads and the hillsides of Palestine.

Mark's Gospel highlights the passionate living of Jesus of Nazareth, the fire that drove him, and the fire he wished to spread on earth. His ministry declares the one discharge from sin and error, which constitute the subtle deadly blighting of lives, ruin the soul of society, and sully the flow of history. Mark shows this passionate élan of Jesus' ministry most succinctly of all: between chapters 1 and 8 of his Gospel he portrays Jesus crash-tackling the four 'plagues' that assault his contemporaries. These are the four 's's': sickness, sin, Satan and spoilt religion.

a. *Sickness.* Having announced the Kingdom of God in the very first chapter, he cures Simon Peter's mother-in-law, a leper, and all the sick and diseased of Capernaum. It is as if he cannot pass by any suffering without 'goodness going out from him' (5:30). With but few exceptions, the healing miracles are not done to prove something, but rather to bring freedom to those whom he encounters.

This freedom will manifest itself in the ability to serve and love those around them. So, for instance, as soon as the fever leaves Simon's mother-in-law, 'she began to wait on them' (1:31). A healthy person becomes a citizen of the Kingdom by loving those around them with concrete deeds.

b. *Sin.* Physical paralysis is one thing, spiritual and moral paralysis is another. Disease may damage and even destroy the body, but the spiritual disease of sin is the ultimate paralysis, since it assaults people at the deepest levels of their humanity, severing their connections with the Creator and others. Sin hits at the highest and deepest. Mark proceeds accordingly in chapter 2 to tell the story of Jesus' encounter with the paralysed man who is lowered through the roof on his stretcher into the presence of Jesus. 'Seeing their faith,' Mark tells us, 'Jesus said to the paralytic, "Your sins are forgiven you" (Mk 2:5). Jesus also heals him physically. Freedom from sin is a far greater freedom than freedom from disease, it is true, but freedom from both is true wholeness.

c. *Satan*. A feature of Mark is Jesus' frequent encounter with 'the unclean spirits.' In chapter 5 there is the dramatic meeting with the man from Gerasa who was possessed by many 'evil spirits.' Mark contrasts vividly the man's earlier condition when 'he would cry out and cut himself with stones' (5:5) with his later condition of being in his full senses and even desirous of staying with Jesus. This desire 'to be with Jesus' (see 5:18) is a proof that he is in the Kingdom of God that has encountered him dramatically in Jesus.

d. *Spoilt Religion*. The ancient Romans had the proverb, 'The corruption of the best is the worst corruption of all'. Jesus meets many expressions of spoilt or corrupted religion. Such religion has the capacity of corrupting to a degree that nothing else could ever match. As such, it would deform its practitioners and make them twice as fit as the inhabitants of Sodom and Gomorrha for hell. Besides, it was a grotesque deformation of the holy religion given to the Patriarchs, clarified by the Prophets, and applied to daily living in Israel's wisdom tradition. Jesus had to reclaim that religion: here we see the fire blaze out in a new way. A striking instance is provided by the argument between Jesus and the Pharisees in Mark chapter 7. The Pharisees had made 'God's word null and void for the sake of [their] tradition' (7:13).

Now someone driven by such fire makes people wonder. Inevitably they ask the question, Who is he? Thus after the calming of the storm, the crowds ask one another, 'Who can this be? Even the wind and the sea obey him' (4:41). As if to highlight this rising amazement, Jesus himself inquires of the

Twelve mid-way through Mark as to who people think he is. When the assembled answers are listed, he puts the same question to the Twelve, 'But you, who do you say I am?' (8:29). Could he be anything less than the Messiah? Peter answers affirmatively, only to show immediately that he had the utterly incorrect notion of the Messiah (8:31-3).

3.2 THE DEATH AND RESURRECTION OF JESUS

The trial and condemnation of Jesus of Nazareth
As Jesus and his mission of inaugurating the Kingdom of God progressed, so too did a gathering opposition to his message. That opposition must have been a particular source of suffering for him. 'He came to his own people, and his own people did not accept him' (Jn 1:12). In rapid succession he foretells three times the rejection he was going to experience. 'The Son of man will be delivered into the hands of men; they will put him to death; and three days after he has been put to death he will rise again' (Mk 9:31; see also Mk 8:31-33; 10:32-34).

With a few strokes of his pen, Mark captures the atmosphere that enveloped the company of the Twelve and the disciples upon hearing this threefold prophecy of the Passion, 'They were on the road, going up to Jerusalem; Jesus was walking on ahead of them; they were in a daze, and those who followed were apprehensive' (10:32).

For the Twelve and the disciples, the prospective of the cross hit with the strength of a sledgehammer, and penetrated to the marrow of the bone with the poignancy of a fiery arrow. And that for two reasons that multiplied each other.

The first was the spectre of the cross. The cross was more than a cruel means of execution: it shouted out the intention of ultimate degradation of the victim. And this was true for both Jews and Romans. The Roman orator, Cicero (104-43 CE), highlights the horrific significance of death by crucifixion in the Roman world (Cicero, *In Verrem*, 66, 170). As for the Jews, the inspired word of God to them had this to say, 'Cursed is everyone who is hung on a tree' (Dt 21:23). The crucified person is put beyond the covenant, beyond all hope of salvation. In a word, the crucified person is a reprobate and damned person in the eyes of Jews and Gentiles.

The second reason had to do with the idea of Messiah. How could the Messiah, the Anointed One, the Holy One of Yahweh, be killed? Worse still, how could he be killed in that unmentionable fashion? Shock and horror gripped the Twelve in hearing Jesus repeat his destiny of death by crucifixion.

Jesus, it seems, accepted the title 'Messiah' when it was given to him. 'He could not deny nor simply repudiate the title "Messiah". But it was an embarrassment to him, and he preferred that it should not be used publicly, until at last his hand was forced' (Dodd, p. 111). Why was it such an embarrassment?

The reason, as hinted at earlier, is the inevitable political and nationalistic colouration of the great ideas and titles forged throughout Israel's bimillennial history. The 'Messiah' was to be the final emissary of the God of Abraham and of the Prophets of Israel, the bearer of his eschatological blessings and, so, the one who will usher in the definitive Kingdom of God on earth. However, 'in the popular mind messiahship was associated with the political and military role of the "Son of David." To play that part was the last thing Jesus desired. Any suggestion that he proposed to do so was a hindrance to his true work and a danger to his cause. His appeal to his people must rest on something other than a debatable claim to messiahship' (Dodd, p. 111).

Here one comes up against a seeming contradiction. 'Does not the assumption that Jesus had an indirect knowledge all along of the saving effect of his death, but said nothing about it, lead to an intolerable contradiction with his proclamation of the Kingdom of God?' If the time had come in truth, and if the Kingdom of God was truly present in Jesus, then how could this be reconciled with the belief that it is only through the death of

Jesus that God brings about the salvation of men? Walter Kasper answers his own question, 'This objection overlooks the fact that the rejection of Jesus' message by Israel as a whole created a new situation... He was forced to make his last journey in lonely anonymity. He was on his own. He made it like all others, in obedience to his Father and for the service of others' (Kasper, p. 121).

In the week of the Passover at the culmination of his 'public ministry', Jesus came to Jerusalem. He entered the Temple and spoke without inhibition. Mark recounts a parable that captures the tone and point of his teaching that from the beginning was always with an authority that could only be explained by a superiority to Moses and an equality with the God of Moses!

> A man planted a vineyard and put a wall around it, hewed out a winepress, and built a watchtower; then he let it out to vine-growers and went abroad. When the season came, he sent a servant to the tenants to collect from them his share of the produce. But they took him, thrashed him, and sent him away empty-handed. Again, he sent another servant whom they beat about the head and treated outrageously... He now had only one to send, his own dear son. In the end he sent him. 'They will respect my son,' he said. But the tenants said to one another, 'This is the heir; come, let us kill him, and the property will be ours.' So they seized him and killed him, and flung his body out of the vineyard (14:1-12).

Mark goes on to say, tellingly, that 'they saw that the parable was aimed at them.' The God of Abraham had indeed sent his prophets to Israel, and Israel had treated them with scorn. Now the beloved Son of God is sent, the Father's final overture and final emissary. Jesus foretells that he, too, will experience the same fate as those who had foretold his coming.

The Jewish and Roman trials

Many scholars have worked on putting together a reconstruction of the sequence of events that led to Jesus' death. There are complex issues that need to be addressed on the basis of the Gospel accounts that have come down to us. Here for the most part we shall follow Gerhard Lohfink's learned and readable *The Last Day of Jesus* (Notre Dame, Indiana: Fortress Press, 1984) and C.H. Dodd's great work, *The Founder of Christianity*, to which we have previously referred.

In John's Gospel we read of a particular meeting of the Sanhedrin, the supreme religious and cultural governing body of Israel, those who 'sat on the chair of Moses'. The discussion was opened by a speaker who drew attention to the fact that Jesus worked signs that were drawing ever greater attention from the people, at the expense of the Scribes and the Pharisees. Worse still, the Romans were likely to intervene with violence against the Holy Place of the Temple and against Jerusalem. The debate was concluded by the High Priest, Caiaphas, who stated quite bluntly, 'You don't seem to have grasped the situation at all; you fail to see that it is better for one man to die for the people, than for the whole nation to be destroyed' (11:49-50).

Jesus knew that his time had come, the hour when he would pass out of this world to the Father and when he would love us to the end (Jn 13:1). He celebrated the Passover, but transformed this central celebration of Israel. He changed the bread into his own Body, and the cup of wine into His Blood (Mk 14:22-26). The Twelve alone are with him. He commands, and therefore also enables them, to do the same: they are ordained as his priests. The institution of the Eucharist is also the institution of ministry in and for the Church (Henri de Lubac, *The Motherhood of the Church*, San Francisco, 1982, p. 340).

The betrayal by Judas occurs immediately. Why did he do this most heinous of deeds, of which his name is long since the personification? Luke simply answers that 'Satan entered

Judas, called Iscariot, one of the Twelve' (Lk 22:3). The troop composed of Temple Guards and militia are guided by Judas to the Garden of Gethsemane. The kiss of Judas identifies Jesus.

Conducted before the Sanhedrin, this first trial had a double purpose. The priests were going to have to discredit Jesus in the eyes of Israel and therefore on religious grounds. The second was to eliminate Jesus by death. And since the Sanhedrin could only pronounce, but not carry out, such a death sentence they would have to have recourse to the hated Roman Governor, Pontius Pilate. A second trial was going to be necessary, then. It would have to convince the Governor that Jesus was a threat to Roman interests since he was on mission to inaugurate a New Kingdom, having spent the three previous years living and proclaiming that very Kingdom.

The Sanhedrin adopted the strategy of asking two questions of Jesus. The first was whether he was the Messiah. The Gospels do not entirely agree about his answer. We know that Jesus would never have applied that title to himself for the reasons that we have mentioned already: Jesus was the Anointed One indeed, but of a kind that was going to be utterly other than the popular politicised version. The second question came again from the High Priest, Caiaphas: 'Are you the Son of God?' St Mark telescopes the two questions together, 'Are you the Messiah, the Son of the Blessed One?' (a synonymn for the name of YHWH which the Jews would not pronounce out of reverence) (Mk 14:61).

Jesus replies, 'I am, and you will see the Son of Man seated at the right hand of the power and coming with the clouds of heaven.' The high priest tore his garments as the standard sign of the sin of blasphemy. 'They all gave their verdict: he deserved to die' (14:64). And there was a further dimension in the charge: Caiaphas had procured a positive reply to the question about the Messiahship of Jesus, and since this had strong political overtones in the society of the day, the priests could go to the Roman trial with a powerful trump card: Jesus claims to be the King of the Jews!

It was Passover time, and nationalist feelings were running high. The governor was in residence in Jerusalem, as was the custom during Passover time. Already three 'bandits' were in prison awaiting execution for their part in an uprising. Their leader was one Barabbas.

Meanwhile, Pontius Pilate interrogated Jesus of Nazareth. The interrogation focused on Jesus' kingship, or rather the kind of kingship that was his. Jesus tells him that his kingship is not of this world; it is not, in other words, based on power or the love of power. Subtly, but dramatically, John's Gospel contrasts the power of love with the love of power.

Realising Jesus' innocence, Pilate most pragmatically has him scourged and crowned and humiliated before presenting him to the populace alongside Barabbas with a popular choice to be made between the two. It was Pilate's gamble. It backfired as, under the canvassing of the Scribes and Pharisees and the priests, the crowd was swayed in favour of Barabbas.

'What shall I do with your king?' The populace, now depersonalised to being a mob, thundered back, 'We have no king but Caesar.' With no way out, Pilate pronounced the deadly sentence, 'You shall climb the patibulum', and so endure the shameful cross. The Saviour of the world had lost a popular vote to a petty brigand and rebel.

Paul's ringing words recur to memory, 'The human race has nothing to boast about to God, for it crucified the Lord of glory' (I Cor 2:8). Perhaps John Henry Newman captures something of the wonder and marvel that happens here when he writes, 'It is the very idea that he is God, which gives a meaning to his sufferings; what is to me a man, and nothing more, in agony, or scourged, or crucified? There are many holy martyrs, and their torments were terrible. But here I see one dropping blood, gashed by the thong and stretched upon the cross, and he is God. It is no tale of human woe which I am reading here; it is the record of the passion of the great Creator' (*Discourses to Mixed Congregations*, London, 1849, p. 321.)

The death-cry of Jesus

The New Testament and Christian Tradition view the death of Jesus profoundly. The German theologian, Walter Kasper, writes: 'It is insufficient to stress the political misunderstanding and the political aspect of his death... For the New Testament Jesus' death is not just the doing of the Jews and Romans, but the saving act of God and Jesus' voluntary sacrifice' (W. Kasper, p. 114).

The mystery of the Cross is a sequence of events beginning with the arrest of Jesus in Gethsemane and concluding with his nailing and three hours of agony on the Hill of Calvary outside the city of Jerusalem (see Heb 13:13) the next day. It is the mystery of the Crucified. There are layers upon layers of theological meaning in this mystery.

There is one aspect of the mystery of Jesus' death on the Cross that is gaining special attention today. If one were asked in former times when Jesus suffered the most, the usual answer was the agony in the Garden of Gethsemane when he prayed, 'Abba! Father! If it is possible take this chalice away. Yet, not my will but yours be done' (Mk 14:36-37). Today there is a different answer: Jesus suffered the most when he cried out, 'My God, my God, why have you forsaken me' (Mk 15:34; Mt 27:46). The summit of Golgotha is the summit of his suffering, and the summit of his suffering is the summit of his loving us. The discovery of this truth was the theological discovery of the twentieth century!

Of the seven last words spoken by our Saviour on the wood of the Cross, the cry of Jesus is the only sentence given by both Mark and Matthew. Mark gives it in Aramaic, Jesus' mother tongue: '*Éloi, Éloi, lama sabachtani*' ('My God, my God, why have you forsaken me?').

It is true that these words are the opening words of Psalm 22 (21). Still, the consensus of biblical scholars and theologians today is that the Psalm was made for Jesus, not Jesus for the Psalm. In other words, it's not simply Jesus praying, but really experiencing this cry of abandonment.

Why the surge of interest in this cry of Our Lord (Mark says that he died 'with a great cry')? The answer is because recent history has witnessed human suffering, particularly that of the innocent such as children, civilians during wars and the starving, to a degree unprecedented in history. After World War II, which saw the mass murder of civilians and of the inmates of extermination camps on a scale hitherto unknown in human history, some theologians and believers wondered if it would be possible ever to speak of God again. But here in this cry, God's eternal Son made flesh seems to gather up in his cry the forsakenness of the whole of humanity, and all this at the summit of his loving of us (see Chiara Lubich, *The Cry*, New York and London: New City, 2001, and Angela Hubbard, 'Psalm 22 and the Paschal Mystery', *The Bible Today*, 36 (1998), pp. 111-116).

Jesus loved us without limits. 'Greater love than this no man has, than that he lay down his life for his friend' (Jn 15:13). On Calvary he offered forgiveness to his executioners, Paradise to the good thief, his mother to St John, and his Father to humanity. And he had the sensation of losing the Father in his human soul. This was the summit of all his suffering.

The cry of abandonment expresses Jesus' experience of his own death. He lived through the loss of his beloved Father in his human soul because, mysteriously, 'it was necessary' (see Lk 24:26) in order for us to enter the Kingdom of his Father.

Attempting to understand the death-cry of Jesus

It is worthwhile to pause a while in order to try to understand this mysterious cry. Why did Jesus experience the abandonment of his Father whom only hours earlier he had with infinite trust and patience addressed as 'Abba'? We will try to enter with reverence into this ultimate wound of his Passion that speaks so profoundly to the men and women of today.

Jesus had come, as he repeatedly said, 'to call the sinners, not the virtuous' (Mt 9:13). We have considered this already. A striking instance of this goal of his whole ministry is to be read in the case of Zacchaeus. Now sinners are by definition without God. They walk away from God 'for the god of this world.' The result is 'godforsakenness'. They move away from God and feel 'godforsaken'. Jesus' seeking out the lost to lead them into the Kingdom of his Father led him to this moment of ultimate solidarity with the lost, in fact, with those who were without God, his Father. He was one with the totally 'godforsaken.'

And being with them in their camp as it were, he lost the sense of the Father's presence in his human soul. This is the abandonment, this is the suffering which is so great that none greater can be thought. Jesus experiences in his human soul the eclipse of his Father. Can we go further in understanding a little what happened? Pope John Paul II invites us to do so. He writes,

> One can say that these words are born at the level of that inseparable union of the Son with the Father, and are born because the Father 'laid upon him the iniquity of us all' (Is 53:6). They also foreshadow the words of St Paul, 'For us God made him to be sin who knew no sin' (2 Cor 5:21). Together with this horrible weight, encompassing the entire evil of turning away from God which is contained in sin, Christ, through the divine depth of his filial union with God, perceives in a humanly inexpressible way this suffering, which is the separation, the rejection by his Father, the estrangement from God (John Paul II's encyclical on suffering, *Salvifici Doloris*, 18).

It is enough to think of how much we revolt at having to put up with a trivial but false accusation to begin to realise the enormity of what the Son of God took on in carrying voluntarily the sins that were lain upon him (see Isaiah 52:12-53:13).

There is a third way to look upon that Face of Sorrow at the heart of the drama. For we must look upon the one we have pierced (Jn 19:34), and ponder in our hearts, as Mary did (Lk 2:19; 51). Jesus came, yes, to bring the Kingdom of God that consists in the restoration of union with his Father and with one another. In a word, he came to give us the Father as 'our Father.' Now when one gives something away out of generosity, one grows in generosity, indeed, but one also loses what one gives. When Jesus loves us and gives himself up for us (Gal 2:20) he has only one purpose in mind: to give us communion with the Father. Therefore, he experiences the loss of the Father for himself in his human soul. That is the abandonment.

This is the ever-greater love that the Scriptures speak about, 'the love of Christ that is beyond all knowing' (Eph 3:18). It means that however far a human being has gone from God, it is not further from God than the eternal Son made man went in his pursuit of us. Every abandoned person, every sinner is 'located' between the abandoned Son and the Father. Indeed, located here too are every division, every lack of reconciliation, every rupture in a relationship. The abandoned are actually placed in that 'in-between' that opens up in the Son's Cry on the Cross.

Jesus crucified and forsaken is the God for our times. We see his face all around us. We see his Face in those who are victims of violence and hatred of any kind: who was more a victim of violence than Jesus? But the whole point is that Jesus Crucified and forsaken is to be found in every suffering. For the abandoned he is refuge. For the lonely he is company. For the failures he is success. For the sinners he is pardon (see 1 Cor 1:30).

It is important to notice that this icon of God, which we see when we 'look upon' the Face of Jesus Forsaken, is unique in the whole world of religion. Here God interprets himself 'for us' in the very depths of suffering and forsakenness. Of course, all ways of religion are an attempt to get beyond the pain and evil of this world. But here in Jesus crucified and forsaken God interprets himself to us in the very depths of suffering and god-forsakenness. 'O all you who pass by, look and see if there is any suffering like unto mine' (Lamentations 1:12).

Scripture tells us that 'No one has ever seen God', it is true, but here, in the forsakenness of Calvary, 'the only Son who is nearest the Father's heart has interpreted him' (Jn 1:18). The Father 'says' who he is to us in his beloved Son 'wounded for our sins and bruised for our crimes' (Is 53:5). Jesus crucified and forsaken is therefore both the Father's self-portrait and the key to the mystery of human existence in all its dimensions, as the Second Vatican Council stressed (see Vatican II, *Gaudium et Spes*, 22).

The Resurrection of Jesus

In chapter two we reflected on the message of Jesus as concentrated in the Kingdom of God. This Kingdom was personified in Jesus himself. Once the tide of popular and ephemeral feeling turned against him, the Kingdom could only come via a final, to-the-death collision with 'the kingdom of this world.' Jesus began his preaching in this fashion and lived it all the way to the shedding of his blood in Jerusalem. His teaching prepared for the Cross, while the Cross manifested the teaching, showing its presence and finality.

The first Christians, however, did not concentrate their message in the Kingdom. Rather, they began with the resurrection of the Crucified Jesus. In his First Letter to the Corinthians, which is among the very first texts of the New Testament, the converted persecutor, Paul, writes that 'if Christ has not been raised [from the dead], our preaching is useless and your believing it is useless.' The Faith stands or falls with the truth of the Resurrection! In fact, 'if our hope in Christ has been for this life only, we are the most unfortunate of all people' (1 Cor 15:14;19). That is why Paul tells the Christians of

Rome that their salvation depends upon believing in their hearts that God raised Jesus from the dead (Rom 10:9).

The preaching of Christ was about the Kingdom of God, but the preaching of the first believers was about Christ's resurrection from the dead. Jesus lived passionately for the Kingdom to the point of the cross and the giving up his own life for it. The preaching of his Apostles proclaims that the Kingdom has in fact arrived through the risen and glorified Christ. As Klaus Hemmerle puts it: 'That Jesus, the crucified, was not left by God in death, but lives and is raised in glory as the Lord is, in the preaching of the Apostles, the sign of the reversal of history itself, a reversal that demands from the hearer of this message a conversion of heart' (Hemmerle, pp. 19, 22).

In the same Letter to his Corinthian converts, Paul provides a statement of the message proclaimed by the Apostles in the very early Church: 'I handed on to you as of first importance what I in turn had received, that

Christ died for our sins in accordance with the scripture,

And that he was buried,

And that he was raised on the third day in accordance with the scriptures,

And that he appeared to Cephas, then to the twelve.' (15: 3-5a)

There are some striking things to be noted about this first creed in the Church. First, it was composed soon after the events it describes, and so predates Paul who hands it on to the Corinthians.

Secondly, it emphasises the two facts of death and of resurrection in such a way as to show that the resurrection reverses the death of Our Lord. In fact, a little while later in the same Letter Paul shouts out, 'Death has been swallowed up victory. Where, O death, is your victory? Where, O death, is your sting?' (15:54-55).

Thirdly, both the death and the resurrection of Jesus are 'in accordance with the scripture', that is, with the Old Testament.

They are hidden in the events, and foretold in the pages, of the Old Testament. That explains why Luke, the close friend of Paul, concludes his Gospel with the story of the risen Lord walking with the two disciples on the road to Emmaus on that first Easter morning, but also walking them through the ages and the pages of the Old Testament, 'beginning with Moses and all the prophets' (Lk 24:27). God fulfils his plan for humanity through the death and the resurrection of his beloved Son.

Finally, there is the fact that the eye-witnesses of the Risen Lord are named: the Church of the Apostles put into her first creed the names of those to whom the crucified Risen Lord actually appeared. The faith will always have to have witnesses: it will not survive on paper as a kind of 'paper religion.' In fact, Paul proceeds to add a list of names to the list: five hundred on one occasion, the Apostle James, all the Apostles, and Paul himself, no doubt referring to the appearance on the road to Damascus.

The Resurrection: God's definitive 'no' to death

What, then, does Christianity say of itself? It does not merely announce truths about God and his works. These truths of course compose 'the noble deposit' of Faith (I Tim 6:20). Rather, it proclaims the intervention of God in history so as to make a new history, since it is a history of 'God with us' (Mt 1:23) – 'an Immanuel history'.

Christianity proclaims a divine and human drama: 'God so loved the world that he gave his only Son' (Jn 3:16) to humankind. It loves to repeat that he came 'to taste death for everyone' (Heb 2:9) and to 'rise on the third day' (Mk 8:31). It proclaims, as its first message and very starting point, that God has spoken a definitive 'No' to our death in all its forms.

How? By the death and the resurrection of his own Son from the tomb where he had been placed by his executioners as a mad and bad blasphemer. The eternal Father would not let his 'Holy One see corruption' (Acts 2:27). The resurrection is the

God of life's definitive 'No' to death in all its forms. It announces that Jesus crashed into and crashed through the worst that his intended beneficiaries could throw at him, especially death on the wood of the cross (Gal 3:13).

What do men and women fear most of all? Principally two items which are in reality one. The first is that they will not be loved and are in fact unlovable in a universe that will not remember once they have left this scene. 'Out of sight, out of mind,' says the proverb. The second fear is that of death, 'the last of the enemies to be overcome' (I Cor 15:26) and the agonising sting it puts into the side of every man and woman. The reality seems to be captured by Patrick Kavanagh in a poem,

> The birds sang in the wet trees,
> And as I listened to them
> It was a hundred years from now
> And I was dead.
> But I was glad
> I had recorded for him the melancholy.

All of man's action and planning consists in the effort to overcome these universal threats. But now the loving Son appears in the world in order to radiate the love of the Father. He comes so that 'we might have life and have it to the full' (Jn 10:10). The Apostles and the first Christians proclaimed this love and lived by this life. A good instance is the Apostle John who opens his First Letter with these words,

> 'Something that has existed since the beginning,
> That we have heard,
> And we have seen with our own eyes;
> That we have watched and touched with our hands:
> The Word, who is life –
> This is our subject.
> That life was made visible:
> We saw it and are giving our testimony,

Telling you of the eternal life
Which was with the Father and has been made visible to us' (I Jn 1:1-2).

The appearances of the Risen Lord in the Gospels

The primitive Christian community employed short confessions of faith, mini-creeds as it were, to proclaim and to announce the death and the resurrection of Christ. Paul, as the first writer of the New Testament, is a special source of these. He stressed the fact of the appearances. This brings us to the central documents of the New Testament, the Gospels. They underline the appearances of the risen Jesus and the Empty Tomb.

The four Gospels provide as many narratives of the appearances of the one who had been crucified (Mk 16:9-20; Mt 28:9-10; 16-20; Lk 24:13-53; Jn 20 and 21). It is impossible to harmonise these accounts with regard to time and place. This is no more an argument against their reliability than the many varying accounts of the causes and course of the French Revolution are an argument against the historicity of the event! What is great and event-like and history-making refuses to be reduced to a neat and compact formula; all the more so, then, an event that was to change the course of history.

The evangelists are convinced that the encounters with the risen Lord took place in the physical order of reality. He could be seen, heard, touched and addressed. In Luke, this is stressed with particular force, 'Why are you so agitated, and why are these doubts arising in your hearts? Look at my hands and feet; yes, it is I indeed. Touch me and see for yourselves; a ghost has no flesh and bones as you can see I have' (24:39-40). The Eleven are the witnesses of 'those glorious unhealed wounds that heal the whole world' (G. K. Chesterton). In the words of Pope John Paul II, 'Like the Apostle Thomas, the Church is constantly invited by Christ to touch his wounds to recognize, that is, the fullness of his humanity' (Apostolic Letter *Novo Millennio Ineunte [At the Beginning of the New Millennium]*, 21).

Still, the risen Christ is not in the condition of his pre-resurrection days. He is not alive or resuscitated as Lazarus was after Jesus raised him from the dead (Jn 11:1-43), nor as the daughter of Jairus (Lk 8:49-56), nor the widow's son of Naim (Lk 7:11-17). All three were still under the power of death, and had to die. But 'death had no more power over Jesus' (Rom 6:8). The Father has raised him into a new order of being, where the divine within him 'streams forth' and 'environs' his humanity (John Henry Newman, *Parochial and Plain Sermons*, Vol. 2, London, 1869).

A new way of being with us
When people hear the word 'resurrection' they are very likely to think of something far less than resurrection. They will reduce it to the level of mere 'physical resuscitation'. The resurrection is something much more wonderful than a mere resuscitation of the crucified body of the Lord. The body that was placed in the tomb has entered into a new order. 'Christ, as we know,' writes St Paul, 'having been raised from the dead will never die again' (Rom 6:8).

The resurrection means that the man Jesus who is the eternal Son of the eternal Father 'lives wholly and for ever in God.' If, in the incarnation, the Son of God left heaven and emptied himself out to take on our humanity – and what a step-down was involved there, more than if you or I could step down to become a little worm on the ground – in the resurrection he took that same humanity that was born of the Virgin Mary and suffered under Pontius Pilate to the right hand of the Father. This is delightfully stated in the hymn that Paul writes into his Letter to the Philippians (2:6-11).

The Gospels bring this out by means of a simple but clever technique: when Jesus appears, the Apostles or the women fail to recognise him until he prompts them by a gesture or a word. The appearance recounted by Luke on the first Easter morning on the Road to Emmaus (Lk 24:13-35) shows this technique in action.

Jesus takes the initiative in 'coming up and walking by the side' of Cleopas and his friend whom St Ambrose (+397 CE) believed to have been his wife. The two disgruntled and downhearted disciples are fleeing Jerusalem while discussing the terrible events of the previous days. Responding to their story, the 'Stranger' takes them through Moses and the prophets to show that 'it was ordained that the Christ should suffer and so enter into his glory' (24:26). Still this was not enough for them to recognise him. There followed the meal in the restaurant in Emmaus; and as they saw Jesus taking, blessing, breaking and giving the Bread 'their eyes were opened and they recognized him' (24:30).

In this account one sees the unvarying structure of each appearance of the Risen Christ. The resurrection 'does not mean distance from the world, but a new way of being with us; Jesus is now with us from God and in God's way; expressed in imagery: he is with God as our advocate, always interceding for us (Heb 7:25)' (Kasper, p. 149).

The Resurrection and hope
St Paul writes that our 'hope is not in vain' (Rom 5:5). The Resurrection speaks of hope. The risen Jesus Christ has lifted our humanity into the eternal presence of his Father. As one of the Fathers of the Church put it, 'God the Son wants to remain a human forever.'

The fact of raising our humanity to God and remaining with us, leading us more and more deeply into God, opens up 'vistas hidden to our minds' (Vatican II, *Gaudium et Spes*, 24). It generates the greatest and most wondrous hope for human beings. As Theo Adorno has written, hope in fact is the only form in which love appears. The poet, G. M. Hopkins, seems to capture this in a poem entitled, 'That nature is a Heraclitean fire and on the comfort of the Resurrection',

> I am all at once what Christ is, since he was what I am, and
> This Jack, joke, poor potsherd, patch, matchwood,

immortal diamond,
Is immortal diamond.

The empty tomb narratives

The devout women who were on Calvary went to the tomb early on Easter morning. All four accounts of the empty tomb agree that they found his tomb empty on the third day after the crucifixion. The story culminates in the kerygma of the resurrection announced by a young man in a white robe in Mk 16:5, by two men in dazzling apparel in Lk 24:4, and by an angel in Mt 28:2.

It is significant in many ways that this message is associated exclusively with women. Women, in fact, could not be witnesses in public courts at the time of Jesus. This fact is a powerful pointer to the truthfulness of these narratives, as well as to the pre-eminent role played by the women disciples of Jesus in the course of Jesus' public ministry and especially during his Passover in love and suffering to his Father and our Father.

The empty tomb does not bring the women of itself to faith in the resurrection. The Gospels describe a variety of reactions from them. Their perplexity turns to faith, however, upon the angelic messengers giving the reason for the absence of the Body, namely, Jesus is risen. Once again it is the appearances that ground faith in the resurrection: the Gospels, like Paul before them (1 Cor 15:3-8), name the recipients of these appearances for the future.

The Empty Tomb narratives are important in that the Apostles would not have been able to proclaim for even one hour in Jerusalem that Jesus was risen from the dead if his body was in the tomb. However, the question as to why the tomb was empty was answered in the appearances. Other explanations were in fact circulated, such as that given in Matthew where the disciples are accused of stealing the body (Mt 28:11-15). And then going on to die as martyrs for what they knew to be untrue!

Jesus as Mediator of Salvation

The events of Jesus' death and resurrection, which along with the Trinity is one of the two principal mysteries of Christianity, shocked the early Christian community. The apostles and the disciples had lived beside Jesus; they had heard his teaching, observed his miracles and felt the attraction of his radiant presence. But they did not understand that he was the only name under heaven by which they could be saved (Acts 4:12), and Jerusalem, and Israel and the whole world. Why was this the case?

The Apostles and disciples had not yet received the Holy Spirit. Human beings cannot bear much reality. That is why Luke concludes his Gospel with the risen Jesus promising the Holy Spirit to the Apostles. He begins his follow-up to the Gospel, The Acts of the Apostles, with the narration of the descent of the Holy Spirit (Acts 2).

In John's Gospel we read that it is the Holy Spirit who leads them into the truth (John 16:13). Some of these truths now begin to shine out, like rays of sun piercing the clouds of dismay and perplexity that had enveloped the Apostles even after the Resurrection.

The Apostles and early communities realised quickly that Jesus was not merely one more messenger from the God of Israel to the children of Israel and to humankind. True, the word of God had been carried down the bi-millennial history of Israel from Patriarch and Prophet to John the Baptist, 'the voice crying in the wilderness' (Is 40:3; Mk 1:3). In the fullness of time, however, there came the fullness of revelation. The eternal Son of the Father descended into human flesh, 'emptying himself out to assume the condition of a slave' (Phil 2:7) and living among us in order to lift us up to God.

In the golden words of Pope Leo the Great (460 CE), 'the incarnation increased what was human, without lessening what was divine', being 'a bending down of compassion, not a lack of power.' ('The Tome of Leo the Great', in Michael O'Carroll,

Verbum Caro: An Encyclopedia on Jesus, the Christ, Collegeville 1982, p. 184)

In the flesh of his Son, the Father had set up the ultimate bond between himself and humankind and the whole of history. Very soon the language of mediator emerged as in the First Letter from Paul to Timothy, 'There is only one God, and there is only one mediator between God and mankind, himself a man, Christ Jesus, who sacrificed himself as a ransom for them all' (2:5).

Left to ourselves we could never reach God. God therefore moved towards us. He loved us to the point of bonding himself with us in 'the new covenant' (1 Cor 11:24). This covenant was sealed in the blood of Jesus whom the Father then lifted up to his right hand. This means that in Jesus the eternal Son of God descends to us, reaching into the depths of our distance from God, in order to lift us up out of our lostness to union with his Father.

In other words, Jesus is the one mediator between God and humankind. St Irenaeus puts it like this: 'It required the Mediator of God and humankind, through His kinship with both, to bring back both to friendship and concord, presenting humankind to God, revealing God to humankind' (*Against the Heresies*, III, 18, 7: translation by John Saward in Hans Urs von Balthasar, *The Scandal of the Incarnation. Irenaeus against the Heresies*, San Francisco, 1990, p. 55).

The variety of images and titles used to describe the risen Lord

Geologists speak of 'the Big Bang' that occurred at the origin of the universe when all the energy then concentrated in one point exploded into action. The result was the phenomenon of the galaxies, the stars and the planets that will always fascinate. The death and resurrection of Jesus to be 'Lord and Christ' (Acts 2:36), together with the sending of the Holy Spirit, constitute the 'Big Bang' of God's dealing with his Creation.

Little wonder, then, that the Gospels and the Apostolic Letters that make up the New Testament abound in titles for the crucified and glorified Jesus. Up to eighty titles have been counted in its pages. Some examples are 'Lord', 'Saviour', 'Son of man', 'mediator', Son of God', and 'New Adam'.

The sheer number of titles for Jesus is an eloquent witness to the wonder of what happened in the event of Jesus Christ and its abiding implications for our lives and for the whole of humankind. Each title is an element in the complete answer to the question that runs through the whole of the New Testament, particularly in the Gospel according to Mark: Who is this Jesus who was crucified and rose again, and who 'raised' others with him to be models of goodness and heroic loving even to death?

The variety of the titles also shows how much our own perceptions need enlarging and correction to understand even a small point of divine revelation: God has to continually remove our puny ideas in order to make way for his idea of himself (Jn 1:18; 1 Jn 4:8ff)! It was of this that Voltaire was thinking when he wrote, 'God made men and women in his image and likeness, and they have certainly got even with him for doing so.' We have our image of God and so often we project false images of God, but God has clarified our images in Jesus Christ, the one closest to the Father's heart (see Jn 1:18).

A new awareness of community
The first and most immediate impact of the events of Easter and Pentecost was the emergence of the Christian Community, the Church. In the words of the German Protestant Martyr, Dietrich Bonhoeffer, 'Jesus did not rise alone: rather he rose as community, because he brought humankind with him.'

The Acts of the Apostles tell us that the first community in Jerusalem 'was one in mind and heart' (4:32), and that they 'remained faithful to the teaching of the apostles, to the brotherhood, to the breaking of bread and to the prayers.' (2:42). In a sense, this description of the early Christian community presents us with four 'sources of God'. Since the God of Jesus Christ is communion, our life in Jesus cannot be merely an individual-centred spirituality but rather a communitarian way to God. The four 'sources' mentioned in this description generate a living communion among the followers of Jesus Christ on earth.

Proof of this community was the fact that the first Christians lived a communion of spiritual and material goods. Accordingly, 'none of their members was ever in want' (4:34). These Christians offered a solution to 'the social problem' by living the communion of goods. How could they be a community in the higher spiritual sense of sharing in the life of the risen Christ when communing with his very Body and Blood in the Eucharist if they were unwilling to be a community also in sharing the humbler daily gifts of their possessions?

The conviction of the first Christians was their experience that the risen and ascended Lord was living among them. They made this discovery quickly: the Holy Spirit far from replacing Jesus, places him among them, in their midst. Matthew's Gospel brings this out clearly. Jesus promises that 'where two or three are gathered in my name, I shall be there with them' (Mt 18:20). John's Gospel too gives us the condition to be fulfilled for this presence to exist. It is summarised in what Jesus calls 'his' and 'new', the New Commandment to love one another (Jn 13:34-5; 15:12). This is to be the typical characteristic of the new Christian community called into life by the Risen Christ.

In his pre-Easter days, Jesus was tied to a particular place and time: now as risen he can be present everywhere and always, in fact wherever any two of his followers want to live by his 'dying wish' of mutual love. This means that today too he can present in factories, parliaments, offices, schools, homes, wherever his followers live by his style of mutual love that is the 'law of heaven', the law of the life of the three divine Persons who love one another, brought on earth.

4
The Formation of Christian Community

Every now and then the Acts of the Apostles provides pen pictures or summaries of what the early Christian community was like. For instance, as we have mentioned before, Luke, in Acts 4:32, describes how the first Christians were 'of one heart and soul' and so shared their goods. The focus was *koinōnia*, a fellowship or communion of life in God and with one another.

Significantly, Luke presents his ideal picture of the Christian community after recounting the descent of the Holy Spirit at Pentecost. It's his way of saying that the unity, mutual love and social expression of this community are not merely a human achievement. It is the Holy Spirit who is at work forming ordinary individuals into a *koinōnia* shaped by the Word, fraternal love and the Eucharist (see Acts 2:42).

The encounter with Jesus Christ did not remove people from the world. They were real people, living real lives in the world. Like everyone else they went about their daily lives bringing up families, trading in business, trying to get on with neighbours in tricky situations, travelling, coping with moral situations that were quite ambiguous, suffering setbacks, grieving over relatives and friends who died, and so on. But through the action of the Holy Spirit their individual stories became part of the great story of a new people born of the Gospel.

In this chapter, we want to look at three of the first communities in some detail. We want to see how did they grow in their understanding of Jesus. What new meaning did they discover from his death and resurrection? How did the social and cultural issues they were faced with help shape their belief and practice in a way that still guides us today?

The three communities we are reviewing (those of Corinth, Thessalonica and Philippi) were established by the apostle Paul. The Apostle of the Gentiles is the great missionary of the new movement that came to life through Jesus' death and resurrection; and the Acts of the Apostles describe his three missionary journeys. This chapter is based, however, on Paul's letters.

The purpose of these pages is not a textual analysis or exegesis of the letters. Instead, it is an attempt, on the basis of the letters, to look through Paul's eyes at these first Christian communities and ask the questions we have just outlined above. We'll see that often it was circumstances, difficulties and controversies that provided opportunities for clarifying key elements of the Christian belief.

The first Christian community of Corinth

In the middle of the first century, Corinth was a thriving city, the capital of the Roman province of Achaia. Although the city of Corinth, with its famous temples and schools, had been destroyed by the Romans in 146 BCE, it was rebuilt as a Roman colony in 44 BCE by Julius Caesar. Many of the colonists living in Corinth in Paul's time were former slaves or freedmen.

Geographically it was well located as it had access to both the Aegean and the Adriatic seas through its two ports Cenchreae and Lechaeum, making it an important crossroads between East and West. This also explains why it had an immense volume of trade. Huge numbers of travellers passed through it. This city, the largest in Greece, was addicted to sporting events and was noted for the Isthmian games, celebrated every second year, and second in importance only to the Olympic games.

An object lesson on the Church in all ages!
When St Paul looked at the Christian community in Corinth, he must have generally felt anguish. 'Christ had sent him to preach the Gospel' (1 Cor 1:17), the Good News of 'the Lord of glory' (2:8). He had indeed brought the Gospel of Christ to Corinth, this busy port, rich in commerce, with a thriving economic life, but noted also for its moral decadence. It seems that an early enthusiasm for the Gospel among the converts in Corinth deteriorated rapidly into problems of exceptional variety and of insoluble texture.

C.K. Barrett writes that 'many winds of doctrine blew into the harbours and along the streets of Corinth, and it must have been very difficult for young Christians to keep on a straight course' (*The Second Epistle to the Corinthians*, London: Adam & Charles Black, 1976, p. 36). It was this very scenario that required Paul to write two Letters: the first was largely rejected and the second is markedly different in tone as the Apostle pleads his way back into the affections of the Corinthian Christians. It is perhaps true to say that the Corinthian Church was Paul's 'heartbreak community'. According to Acts 18:11, Paul stayed in the city a year and six months.

The spectacle that greeted the Apostle's eyes was both multi-coloured and often negative. That is why a study of this letter is fascinating from so many points of view.

First of all, we can see an Apostle wrestling with a fledgling community that had heard the Gospel of the glory of Christ (1 Cor 2:8) only years before and within a decade or two after the events of Christ's death and resurrection.

An examination of this fledgling community is worthwhile also because it brings out the sheer variety of the problems in the Church of Corinth. These problems were theological, doctrinal, moral, liturgical, organisational and existential.

Thirdly, these difficulties show us the life of a struggling early community and the ministry of an Apostle in that very setting. That ministry is received from the Lord (1:1) and, as such, enjoys the highest authority. However, it has to be exercised in the concrete.

Fourthly, Corinth was a community that had considerable hesitation in accepting the apostolic structure of the early Church, in particular the prophetical, priestly and governing functions of the Apostle Paul. It prided itself on its very charismatic dimensions.

In a word, to study the early apostolic church of Corinth is to do an object lesson on the Church in all ages! As Barbara Bowe puts it: 'The social and religious differences that troubled Christians in Corinth persist in similar ways among us today. Everywhere today we encounter a great variety among people and their divergent views – in our families, our place of work, our schools and parishes, and in the civic communities we call "home"... We know the demons that plague such efforts to build community in our day: racial hatreds, economic differences, the clash of values and the difference in worldviews... It was no different in the time of St Paul' ('Paul and First Corinthians', *The Bible Today*, 35 (1997), p. 268).

Divisions and Christ Crucified
Perhaps the root cause of the troubles in the church of Corinth is to be found in the open disunity that is rampant in Corinth. '... there are quarrels among you. What I mean is this: each of you is saying, "I am for Paul", or "I am for Apollos"; "I am for Cephas", or "I am for Christ"' (1:11-12). News of these serious divisions in the community had reached Paul from 'Chloe's people' who had returned from Corinth to Ephesus where he wrote the letter.

Paul identifies this disunity as the most open wound in this community he had evangelised. His thought is forthright, 'Surely Christ has not been divided!' And the practical rhetorical conclusion, 'Thank God, I never baptized any of you, except Crispus and Gaius' (1:12, 13, 14; see 3:1-9).

This is quite a vigorous salvo to fire at the very outset of his letter: it was hardly likely to endear Paul to the community, and goes a long way towards explaining the recalcitrant reception by the Corinthians. One can almost hear them muttering angrily, 'Who does this Paul think he is?' But Paul is convinced. For him, the unity of believers in Christ through *agape*-love is not merely desirable, it is essential for the health of the whole Body of Christ.

'Am I to come to you with a rod in my hand, or with love and a gentle spirit?' (4:21). The tension felt by Paul is palpable. Yet he must speak the truth, and 'proclaim Christ nailed to a cross' (1:23), and 'do it without recourse to the skills of rhetoric, lest the Cross of Christ be robbed of its effect' (1:17).

The crucified but now glorious Christ is everything. And when the early Christian community of Corinth read this letter they will have been in no doubt about this. Paul uses this opportunity as a teaching moment: 'God has made him our wisdom, and in him we have our righteousness, our holiness, our liberation' (1:30).

This verse is arguably the most important line in the whole of St Paul. What an irony that it should emerge in such a troubled and fractured setting! Perhaps it is only when there is trouble in the Church that the further reaches of divine revelation are unpacked and the Good News of Christ is noticed!

Need to change mindset
In fact, Paul wants all to realise that 'Christ nailed to a cross… is the power of God and the wisdom of God' (1:23-4). In any case, this is the reminder Paul trots out to his converts as he explains to them what drove him during his ministry among them, 'I resolved that while I was with you I would not claim to know anything but Jesus Christ – Christ nailed to a cross' (2:2).

As Saul of Tarsus, Paul had persecuted those 'belonging to the Way' (Acts 9:2), as the very first Christians were called. God's merciful love, however, had overlooked his persecuting of the Church of God (see 1 Cor 15:9). No doubt part of his strong words written to these first Christians was due to the idea of a crucified Messiah. Learned rabbi that he was, he knew the Old Testament inside out. He knew the saying in Deuteronomy, 'Cursed be the man who hangs on a cross' (Dt 21:23). How could the expected Messiah come to such a fate?

His experience on the road to Damascus had changed all that radically and forever. He discovered that the crucified Jesus was risen, that he was the longed for Messiah, that he was the very equal of the God of the Old Testament, and that he loved us to the point of going to the shameful death on the cross. To communicate this news to his former co-religionists and to the pagans was to take on the most dramatic of all missions.

In Corinth, Paul encountered two impenetrable mindsets, the one 'Greek', the other 'Jewish'.

For the Greeks, wisdom was the reward of a long search for the meaning of life: it involved the climb up from this world towards the realms of truth and beauty in the beyond. But the crucified now exalted Christ had 'climbed down' to the lowest of all places, death on a cross.

For the Jews, their history spoke of God's 'mighty deeds'. Accordingly they understood that mighty signs and divine interventions were necessary to change everything here below: could the idea of a crucified God ever make sense to them?

One can imagine Paul going forth with the fire of the Good News in his heart and still saying something like, 'Humanly speaking, neither Jew nor Greek ought to believe me, but how divine it would be if they did! What a gift it would be for them to understand the crucified Christ! Then they would know "what no eye has seen, nor ear heard, nor the heart of man ever imagined, all God has in store for those who love him" (1 Cor 2:9).' Paul's sorrow, even anguish, consisted in the fact that the

Corinthians did not see and did not hear and did not realise in their hearts 'the length and the breadth, the height and the depth' of this goodness. They had not come 'to know the love of Christ which is beyond all knowing' (Eph 3:19). This is the key to the message of Paul. It also shows us his perspective in the two Letters, enabling us to appreciate the particular solutions he provides to the many problems in Corinth.

Problems become teaching opportunities
Here, as in other letters, Paul takes the concrete issues that have arisen in the community and gives clear direction on how to apply the light of Jesus Christ to these situations.

First, there is sexual immorality among the Corinthians (1 Cor 5). They forget that the 'body is a temple of the Holy Spirit who dwells in them' (6:19). In the incarnation, human flesh had walked into divinity by the front door: the whole person, body, soul and spirit, had been exalted. Chastity was the recognition of this truth and dignity, fornication its denial.

Then there was the fact of lawsuits taken by Christians to the pagan courts: Paul points out the scandal of Christians fighting with one another in the pagan courts.

Chapter 7 deals with marriage, and virginity as 'marriage to the Lord'. Without the love of the Lord, neither can flourish. Paul shows solid support for married and family life and, at the same time, he emphasises the radical difference that the resurrection of Christ has made in our perception of time and history and how this impacts on the Christian vision of marriage and virginity (see Carolyn Osiek, 'First Corinthians 7 and Family Questions', *The Bible Today*, 35 (1997), pp. 275-279).

Another major issue was how to integrate the new life in Christ with the practices of the surrounding culture. The particular question was whether it was lawful for the converts in Corinth to eat the food offered to the idols in the pagan sacrifices. Paul's solution is in terms of the wisdom that is born of love: you are free to eat, still do not employ that freedom if doing so you scandalise others.

The theme of freedom fascinated Paul, that deep freedom from sin and wrongdoing that effectively enslave you. Paul sees freedom as a freedom 'for' and so to be exercised in favour of others who are my brothers and sisters 'for whom Christ died.' (8:11). This notion of freedom has implications for the way the new Christian community is to express the novelty of life in Christ at all levels from gender issues to coping with not shocking their neighbours!

For instance, their new freedom in Christ would have said that it is perfectly okay for Christians to eat the meats offered to the idols in the pagan sacrifices. Nevertheless, the true freedom of love suggested going along with their wish not to eat this meat and so avoid scandalising them. The less perfect in unity is better than the more perfect in disunity!

Once again, Paul underlines *agape*-love, not simply the sentiment of love or altruistic almsgiving. No, the agape-love Paul talks about is that shown and communicated in Christ, the charity that gives us eyes to see, as St Thomas Aquinas, the famous theologian, would put it centuries later.

The Eucharist
First Corinthians gives a mini-treatise on the Eucharist in chapters 10 and 11. The Eucharist, after all, explains charity. The Eucharist is the Saviour's Body that is given for us and his Blood that is shed for us (11:24-5). It is the warm love of the Saviour. The Eucharist makes the many into one Body, the Body of Christ spread out in space and time. 'We, though many, are one body because we all partake of the one holy food' (10:17).

From this fact there flows the imperative of mutual love. That's why it's a scandal when at their Eucharistic celebrations the rich members of the community at Corinth look down upon the poor in practice (11:17-22). They are failing to recognise their equal dignity as the members of Christ's 'eucharistised' Body.

Most of the named Christians in Paul's first letter to the Corinthians appear to be prominent and wealthy people. In particular, Gaius has a house large enough to accommodate the whole church in Corinth (Rom 16:23; 1 Cor 1:14). Others from the upper social strata in Corinth include Crispus (1 Cor 1:14), the 'ruler of the synagogue' (Acts 18:8), Stephanus (1 Cor 16:15, 17; 1:16), Erastus (Rom 16:23), Phoebe (Rom 16:3), Priscilla and Aquila (Acts 18:2-3; 1 Cor 16:19; Rom 16:3-4). In all probability these were also the most influential members of the Church.

Yet, it is clear from 1 Cor 1:26-29 that the majority of the Church were not from the upper social stratum of the time, i.e. those who were 'wise... powerful... of noble birth'. Some were slaves at the time of their calling (7:21; 16:15), and Paul can refer to some in the Church as 'those who have nothing' (11:22).

What Paul emphasises in this first letter to the Corinthians is that the Eucharist implies mutual love regardless of one's social class or category. Once again, we see controversy over this very issue becomes the context for a rich teaching on the doctrine of the Eucharist.

The gifts of the Spirit and the great lesson of love
The criterion of *agape*-love comes into view again as Paul deals with the gifts that the Spirit has poured out upon the Corinthians. Instead of building up the Church of Corinth in the strong bonds of mutual love, the way these gifts were received by the Corinthians had become a source of tension.

This leads Paul to what is perhaps the summit of the first Letter, the moving hymn to charity. 'I may speak in tongues of men or of angels, but if I have no love, I am a sounding gong or a clanging cymbal... I may have faith enough to move mountains; but if I have no love, I am nothing... Love is patient and kind. Love envies no one, is never boastful, never conceited, never rude... Love will never come to an end' (13:1,2,4-5,8).

It's the great lesson that this community of Corinth has to learn about Christian community. The Christian is called to be the copy or prolongation of Christ, and Christ is Love, the ecstatic love of the Father that stands forth in the world. 'Make love your aim', Paul adds (14:1). Not only to love, but to become love, is the DNA for human and Christian living.

Death and Resurrection
If Paul reaches heights of faith-insight in the hymn to charity in chapter 13, he does the same in his moving treatment of the death and resurrection of Jesus in chapter 15. Once again the stimulus to his writing seems to be serious doctrinal aberration in the community: some of the Corinthians deny 'the resurrection of the dead' (12).

This denial, however, means the denial of the resurrection of Christ, and 'if Christ was not raised from the dead, your faith is in vain and you are still in your sins' (15:17). Paul's strategy is to remind the Corinthians of the Gospel he received and in turn handed on to them (15:1).

This conclusion of the first chapter contains what is perhaps Paul's most startling formulation of the 'good news': in his death on the Cross, the Son of God has taken the humanity in which he suffered to the right hand of the Father. In doing so, he has also taken your humanity and mine with him.

This is the meaning of Christ's resurrection. The Father has spoken his definitive 'No' to death in all its forms. While death is the stinging thorn in the side of humanity, now there is a new charge for humanity, both individually and collectively – to share body and soul in the risen life of Christ. 'O Death, where is your sting?... Thanks be to God! He gives us victory through our Lord Jesus Christ' (15:55, 57).

The second letter: the beauty of the Crucified Christ
The reaction to Paul's first letter on the part of the Corinthian Church was so negative that Paul had to write a second letter, a

'letter which came out of great distress and anxiety; how many tears I shed as I wrote it!' (2 Cor 2:4). This letter has been lost (2:3-4 and 7:8).

The existing 'Second' Letter was then written perhaps in two instalments. In the first instalment (chapters 1-9), Paul urges forgiveness and reconciliation in the community. He also paints a positive portrait of the Christian life enjoyed by the Corinthians despite sufferings of all kinds.

But again we see how Paul is fascinated by the splendour-beauty of the crucified and risen Christ. As at the outset of the First Letter, so here once more he holds up this same crucified and glorified love as a mirror for the Corinthians, 'For the God who said, "Out of darkness let the light shine", has caused his light to shine in our hearts, the light which is knowledge of the glory (beauty) of God on the face of Jesus Christ' (2 Cor 4:6).

Christ is the eternal Beauty of the eternal Father. That Beauty, however, must be 'seen' by Christians. When it is, they will be drawn to be followers, and not merely admirers from a distance.

In this second letter Paul links the *koinōnia* to which the community is called with the wisdom that comes from the Crucified Christ. It is the wisdom-knowledge acquired through suffering that builds up the *koinōnia* (see Veronica Koperski, 'Suffering, *Koinōnia* and Wisdom in 2 Corinthians', *The Bible Today*, 37 (1999), pp. 139-144).

Paul's apostolic mandate
The proud Corinthians, however, were in revolt against 'the apostle of Jesus Christ by God's will' (1:1). That explains the fact that the second instalment of the Letter (chapters 10-13) is a lengthy *apologia* for Paul's apostolic ministry. Paul is driven to show his credentials as an authentic apostle. 'The signs of an apostle were there in the work I did among you, marked by unfailing endurance, by signs, portents and miracles' (12:12).

It is important to appreciate the meaning of this extraordinary justification of Paul's apostolic mandate. Paul is not concerned to pull rank, to lord it over the Corinthians or to curry favour with them. Rather his concern is to remain in vital and life-giving contact with the Christians of Corinth so that the good news, the graces and the sacramental gifts, all of which the risen Lord has given to him for them, will in fact reach them. If they will no longer accept the apostolic mandate of Paul, then they will fail to receive the Lord's own gifts!

Conclusion

Reflecting back over the two Letters to the Corinthians, certain things stand out more than others.

Most of all perhaps the dominant features of the early Church emerge with clear contours. That Church was founded on a definite 'good news' or 'Creed', 1 Cor 15 being a shining instance. And, as Raymond Collins comments, Paul 'challenged the Corinthians to allow the Gospel to engage them in the warp and woof of their daily lives' (*First Corinthians* (Sacra Pagina, Vol. 7), Collegeville: Liturgical Press, 1999, p. 29).

Next, the Church was sacramental: the sacrament of baptism was foundational (1 Cor 1:13-17), and the sacrament of the Eucharist constitutive of the life of the community with its resultant ethical imperatives (1 Cor 11).

Thirdly, the community received its Creed and its sacraments from an Apostle who reminded them that neither Creed (1 Cor 15:1-3) nor Sacrament (1 Cor 11:23-25) originated with him but from the Lord himself. Paul, however, enjoyed the mandate of Christ to teach that Creed in Christ's name and to oversee the sacraments with the same authority. In a word, the Church was Apostolic. The very 'charismatic' Church of Corinth was doctrinal, sacramental and apostolic in structure.

This latter dimension continued, however, to be a cause of resentment towards Paul. Within three decades of Paul, the Bishop of Rome, Clement, had to intervene dramatically in the context of a schism within the church of Corinth. His letter, which has come down to us, names the rejection of 'the presbyters' of the Church as the nature of the schism. The third successor of St Peter intervened to compose authoritatively the split produced by this schism. It seems as if some Corinthians had finally repudiated essential elements of what the Apostle of the Gentiles did and taught.

The community of the Thessalonians

The city of Thessalonica was founded by Cassander, one of the generals of Alexander the Great in 315 BCE. This city, named in honour of Cassander's wife, the half-sister of Alexander the Great, was the capital of the Roman province of Macedonia and the seat of the governor of that province.

Situated on the *Via Egnatia*, the main route across the Balkans, the city was a major naval station, commercially very active and so attracted a cosmopolitan population. It was the most populous city of Macedonia and one of the larger cities in the Roman Empire, so it was an important and strategic centre for the spread of the Faith in Macedonia.

According to the Acts of the Apostles, Paul, Silvanus and Timothy came to Thessalonica during Paul's second mission and Paul probably stayed there for a few months. Paul's letter to them seems to have been written early on during his time at Corinth around 50 CE, just a few months after he had left Thessalonica. The first letter to the Thessalonians is the first of all of Paul's letters and as such is the first of a small library of writings that would become the sacred writings of the New Testament.

What we are seeing in Paul's letters to the Thessalonians is a very young community. They give us a glimpse into the issues and questions facing the community at this time. Raymond F. Collins comments that the letter 'provides the oldest literary evidence of the significance attached to the death and resurrection of Jesus by the early Christians' ('The First Letter to the Thessalonians' in Raymond Brown, Joseph Fitzmyer and Roland E. Murphy eds., *The New Jerome Biblical Commentary,* London: Geoffrey Chapman, 1993, p. 773).

The positive situation of the believers in Thessalonica
From the letter to the Thessalonians we get a sense of the make-up of the community. When Paul arrived there, Thessalonica had an important Jewish community with its synagogue. But the reference to the Thessalonians having turned from 'idols' (1 Thes 1:9) indicates that the newly formed church is a predominantly Gentile-Christian community. The treatment of the theme of manual trades in 1 Thessalonians (4:11) may suggest that the majority of church members belonged to the working (middle or lower) class.

During his stay among them, Paul had probably won many of them to Christ during his own work at his trade at a shop in the market place (2:9). He had been gentle among them 'like a nurse taking care of her children' (2:7) and 'like a father with his children' (2:11). Paul shared his own life and experience and it was this 'gospel of God' that made an impact on them. However, because of 'great opposition' (2:2), due to envy at the success of his mission (Acts 17:5), Paul and his companions were forced to leave the city much sooner than they would have chosen (1 Thes 2:17).

Having moved on to Athens and, being unable to return himself to Thessalonica, Paul dispatched Timothy to go to the church at Thessalonica 'to strengthen and encourage' them (6 3:2). When Paul met Timothy again after he returned from his visit, Timothy's news of the church in Thessalonica was very heartening. According to the letter, Timothy brought 'the good news of your faith and love' (3:6).

If love of neighbour is a hallmark of Christian existence (Rom 12:10; Jn 13:34; 15:12,17), then the first letter to the Thessalonians is evidence of this. What comes across is the intensity of genuine love that existed between Paul and the community. Paul says that he would gladly communicate not only the Gospel but also his soul, thoughts and feelings, indeed his very life with them (1 Thes 2:8). He wants to hear news of them and 'lives again' when he hears they are doing well. Likewise, we are told they are eager to see him again (3:6-8).

The questions
In spite of Timothy's positive report, this is a young community that continues to need Paul's pastoral care and guidance. They are a fledgling community living in a hostile environment. Timothy reported that the Judaising group was trying to discredit the authority of the three missionaries. And he also brought two questions to Paul's attention that were disturbing members of the community, one concerning the date of the Parousia or Second Coming and the second on the fate of their brothers and sisters who had died before the Parousia.

A Church
The opening verse of this letter describes the group of believers as a Church (in Greek *ekklesia* [1:1]). The word for Church comes from the Hebrew term (*Qahal*) used in the Old Testament for the sacred assembly of the chosen people.

The new Church-community of Thessalonica builds on that chosen people. And yet this community is 'chosen' also in the sense that God loves them immensely in providing a new 'living space', as it were. They are a people who live 'in God the Father and the Lord Jesus Christ'. This is interesting in terms of doctrine because Paul is teaching the equality of Jesus Christ and God the Father.

With these simple words of introduction, the apostle is also making the point that what links the members of this new community is not just politics, social environment, race or friendship but rather the fact that they inhabit a new world, the one created by the Gospel of God the Father's love of them in Jesus Christ.

A few verses later, the Holy Spirit is also indicated as the hidden protagonist in building up the early Church. It was because of the Holy Spirit that the Thessalonians experienced 'joy'. The Spirit who led the earthly Jesus and inspired Paul was with the Thessalonians in power (1:4-6), bringing a deep conviction that God was actively present in them.

A model community
Thanksgiving is the hallmark of the first two chapters of this letter. Such was the overwhelming experience of the Risen Christ who lived among them, that the early Christians were characterised by an enormous sense of gratitude to God. Paul too is grateful for what he has seen and witnessed come to life among this new community. He remembers their faith, love and hope (1:2-3). Once again these are not human achievements but what God has brought about in them through grace.

Paul notes the perseverance of this new community of Thessalonica. Just as it was for Paul, so too for the members of this new community, following Jesus meant affliction (1:2), but, faced with difficulties, they remained steadfast.

The point is, however, that in Christianity you cannot go to God alone. It is a communitarian adventure. So we read that the community at Thessalonica was helped to remain faithful to the Gospel because the members had good models such as Paul and his companions (1:6). The community in turn itself became a model for the newly founded communities in the whole area of Macedonia and Achaia (northern and southern modern Greece) because of its fidelity to Jesus (1:7-8).

Need to improve
While the community of Thessalonica was commended by Paul for having believed in the Gospel, not as a human invention but really 'the word of God' (2:13), its members also found they had to continue and improve in putting this into practice! The Christian community life can never be static. It must be dynamic, growing, progressing, developing. This

explains why Paul reminds them that believing is a fundamental choice, a total commitment (1:9). In a spirit of mutual encouragement, Paul prays that 'they increase and abound in love to one another and to all' so that they might be established in holiness (3:12-13). It is also clear from 4:13-18 that Paul judges they have to grow in the virtue of hope that Jesus has triumphed and banished despair and sadness (4:13).

The second coming
The major issue facing this community revolved around Christ's second coming (4:13-5:11). It seems that this early Christian community believed that Christ would soon return to bring about the consummation of all things. But the problem was that some members of the community had died already before the second coming. In a state of shock, those members of the community who were alive were asking if those who had died would be excluded from the triumph of Christ.

This confusion, difficulty and shock became the occasion for Paul to clarify some points of doctrine. His reply was that, alive or dead, we are all united to Christ. Those who have already died in Christ will also rise and meet him when he comes in his glorious return (4:13-18).

Paul indicates the need for them to be ready for 'the day of the Lord'. It seems that Paul himself hoped for the coming of the Lord soon, although it is probably more accurate to say he stressed the unexpectedness of Christ's coming rather than its nearness: 'the day of the Lord will come like a thief in the night' (5:2). It is also the case that in the second Pauline letter to the Thessalonians we read that the second coming will not be immediate.

Use of apocalyptic imagery
What's interesting to note is that, in teaching the Thessalonians on this topic of the second coming, Paul uses ideas current in Jewish apocalyptic writings about the glorious coming of the

Messiah and metaphorical imagery of various Old Testament theophanies. The imagery such as the 'archangel's call' and 'sound of the trumpet of God' and being 'caught up together... in the clouds to meet the Lord in the air' is symbolic, communicating profound truths concerning the second coming. The symbolism would have been familiar to many of the hearers of these words.

Likewise, in the second letter, ideas such as the appearance of the Rebel or Enemy or a Great Revolt or Apostasy to take place before the final coming are references from Jewish apocalyptic writings. The people of Israel looked forward to a Messiah who would inaugurate the last times by his coming. It would be a time of triumph and majesty preceded by a series of events. The Christian claim was that Jesus inaugurated the last times, but the ultimate triumph and majesty were still in the future.

Lifestyle issues
What comes across loud and clear from the experience of this Thessalonian community is that the belief in the resurrection and the Lord's second coming can never be an excuse to lapse into a lazy waiting game. In fact, Paul tells the Thessalonians straight out: 'this is the will of God, your sanctification' (4:3), in other words, they are to be attached to God and what God wants of them in this life.

The impact of faith touches on all aspects of life. It means keeping to God's plan for human sexuality, something that would have meant going against the current. Furthermore, the idleness of some in the community was bringing hardship to others (4:11-12; 5:14). Paul advises them to go on working, earning a living, avoiding idleness. He also advises them to live in love, peace and harmony with the leaders in the community (5:12-14).

Paul's emphasis on rendering visible the new lifestyle that comes from following and living the Word of God is also in view of impacting on the socio-religious milieu of the Thessalonian world. There were numerous religious cults in

Thessalonica. Paul wants the community's life of holiness to be an example to the non-Christian outsiders. Earl Richard writes: 'one should attribute Paul's concern in this correspondence for social issues and treatment of outsiders as owing to the Thessalonian milieu wherein a major politico-religious concern was the honouring of the deities and patrons who contributed to the city's well-being. The new converts were to do their share in social and economic terms and conduct themselves properly in the company of their neighbours' (*First and Second Thessalonians* [Sacra Pagina], Collegeville: Liturgical Press, 1995, p. 3).

The Christian community of Philippi

Philippi, a city in north-eastern Greece was about ten miles from the Aegean Sea. Its background tells us something of its make up. The name 'Philippi' came from King Philip II of Macedon, father of Alexander the Great. After Rome conquered Macedonia in 168-167 BCE. King Philip made this city a major centre on the *Via Egnatia*, a highway that connected Asia Minor (modern day Turkey) and Italy. Over time it emerged as a leading town in the province of Macedonia.

Philippi became quite famous after Anthony and Octavian defeated Brutus and Cassius in 42 BCE on the plane near the city. Subsequently this urban centre received the honour of becoming a Roman colony and was governed by Italian law. Soon, a sizable colony of Italians filled the city adding to the numbers of the native population. The new immigrants brought with them the Roman language and customs.

It was in this city that Paul, on his second missionary journey, founded his first European Christian community (Acts 16:12-40). He had been directed in a dream to evangelise Europe. The initial success of his mission here was due in large measure to the role played by women such as Lydia, possibly Paul's first convert on European soil, and others such as Euodia and Syntyche.

The city lacked a Jewish synagogue. But there was a 'place of prayer' (Acts 16:13) just outside the city near the river Crenides. It seems the Christian community developed largely among Gentiles.

Paul developed a very close relationship with this community and it was possibly his favourite one (see Phil 1:3-4, 9-11). Its members supported his work after he had left them. As he reminds them, 'Even when I was in Thessalonica, you sent me help for my needs more than once' (4:16).

Philippi was not far from another great city of that time – Ephesus. And it is quite possible that Paul wrote letters, including this one, from Ephesus where he was imprisoned for some time. Likewise, Paul, a sensitive and loving apostle, wrote to them from Thessalonica, a city where he arrived shortly after his time in Philippi.

Paul's letter to the Philippians shows (1:1-2) that in the 50s of the first century CE the church at Philippi was structured. It had *episkopoi* (overseers-bishops) and *diakonoi* (ministers-deacons).

Mary Ann Getty comments that in Paul's letter to the Philippians, a very early document within the New Testament, 'we meet Paul the human being who aches for a church experiencing painful divisions, a church in need of healing and encouragement' (*Philippians and Philemon*, Dublin: Veritas, 1980, p. 73).

A culture of giving
One of the first features that we notice about this Christian community from Paul's letter is a culture of giving which marks these Christians out as special. The community may have been living a communion of goods similar to that described in Acts 4:32. This sharing of wealth extended to sending money to Paul in prison through one of the members of the community, Epaphroditus. They also sent help to him in Thessalonica. The immediate reason for writing the letter to the Philippians was to thank them for their gift to him in a time of need.

This social action on the part of the Philippians wasn't mere philanthropy. Paul calls it a 'fragrant offering' (Phil 4:18). In other words, their culture of giving and communion of goods were part of the very fabric of being a Christian.

Paul indicates that Christians living this culture are involved in a dynamic that involves God. Central to Christian faith is the belief that we have a Father who cares for us, lovingly watching over every detail of our lives. So, in commenting on how the Philippians have been generous in giving, he goes on to assure them that God too does his part: 'And God will supply every need of yours' (4:19).

Paul's references to money, wealth and its use is dealt with in the context of some specific situation the Christians are facing. A Scripture scholar, Carolyn Thomas, summarises his message: 'Generous sharing of one's resources elicits the generosity of God. Use of wealth to advance the cause of the Gospel renders a kind of worship of God' ('Economic Issues in Paul', *The Bible Today*, 32 (1994), p 294).

How the community is formed

This letter also informs us how the early Christian communities were built up and formed. In a certain sense, it was formed from the sharing of spiritual insights and experience that Paul had personally gained from living the Gospel.

We read of Paul having 'learned the secret of facing plenty and hunger, abundance and want' (4:12). He communicates this experience and wisdom to the community. He teaches by sharing his experience.

For Paul, to be a member of the Christian community isn't about being either rich or poor; it's about how you live through the situation you are in. If you are poor, you trust in God and make your need known and are open to how God's providence may arrive. If you are rich, you give to those in need. As Paul wrote in another letter to Corinthians, for Christians it's 'a matter of equality' (2 Cor 8:13).

A community facing adversity

A big issue in this community was how to face adversity (Phil 1:28). It seems that they were experiencing considerable antagonism from fellow citizens.

For a start, the values and lifestyle of the community were at odds with that of the surrounding culture.

Paul was also aware of a threat from Christians of a Jewish background who were not members of this Church (3:2-4). It appears that they were seeking to impose practices such as circumcision on the Gentile Christians of this Church (i.e. those who became Christians without having been formed by the First Testament). They preached a higher 'perfection' (3:12-16), but based on a system that for Paul was now outdated.

Paul first of all pleads with the Christians of Philippi to be an example for others. He calls on them to 'do everything without grumbling or questioning' so that they might be 'blameless and innocent, children of God without blemish in the midst of a crooked and perverse generation, among who you shine as lights in the world, holding fast the word of life' (2:15-16).

Paul also exhorts them to see what is positive in the culture around them. There are indeed values in the culture they can embrace in common with their fellow citizens. He writes 'whatever is true, whatever is honourable, whatever is just, whatever is pure... think about these things' (4:8).

Nevertheless, Paul responds also to the concrete difficulties of antagonism that members of the community are feeling. He does so by telling again of his own experience. He too has his critics and even knows what prison is like because of others' 'envy and rivalry', 'selfish ambition' or 'contentiousness' (1:7, 15-17; 3:2). Added to the physical hardship of prison, the fact that some Christians were criticising Paul meant he had to endure mental distress as well. Added to all of that was the fact that the apostle was possibly facing execution!

Paradoxically, all of these painful circumstances helped Paul to address the situation in which the young community of

Philippi found itself. He takes his own first hand experience as an example to show that even suffering can be a springboard for launching the Gospel of Jesus Christ. His imprisonment 'in Christ' has in fact become a vehicle for influencing people outside the Church. It turns out that the whole 'praetorium' (the imperial governor's residence) came to know about Jesus because of Paul's imprisonment (1:13).

Not only that but it seems that other members of the Christian community itself had now gained new courage to stand up for their faith and speak the word of God. In other words, the Gospel went ahead. Even imprisonment contributes (1:12)! Paul is able to point to the providential, loving hand of God that guides everything, always, and in all circumstances, even imprisonment! So the Philippians aren't to be afraid because 'it is God who gives you the victory' (1:28).

In fact, now that suffering has come their way, Paul encourages them to see it as a 'privilege' as they can suffer for Christ in the Christian 'battle' that Paul too keeps fighting (1:30). The difficult circumstances of the community have been the opportunity to deepen their understanding of Jesus and evangelisation.

The importance of joy

The paradox of Christianity shines out in this letter because despite all the difficulties Paul gives witness to the deep joy that the Gospel brings him in the midst of all his sufferings. In fact, this letter is full of references to joy (1:18,25; 2:2,27-29; 3:1; 4:1). Joy became one of the typical features of the early Christian communities. Everyone searches for happiness. Christians who live the Gospel have joy. But the lesson from Paul to the community is clear. He wants them to bring the Gospel to others and to do so with joy. The difficulties they are going through can be the means for spreading the Good News. Certainly, evangelisation passes through the Cross; but, because of Jesus Christ and the Spirit, difficulties can be transformed into joy.

Facing death

The imminent possibility of death for Paul himself also becomes the occasion for him to help the community grow in its understanding of the significance of Jesus' death and resurrection for facing our own death (1:20-26). Paul shares his inner thoughts and soul with regard to this important question.

How does he see death? His response is clear: it would be a gain because it brings an even greater closeness to Christ. By offering this short reflection to the community Paul simply wants them to reflect on what it means to 'depart this life and be with Christ' (1:23).

It has been said that the general context of Paul's reflection on living and dying may be the Greek and Latin ideas about life and the flesh as burdens from which to be freed. In other words, some philosophies of that time had a negative view of our body and the world. But that doesn't tally with belief in Jesus Christ. Paul doesn't consider this life a prison from which we should be released. No. The whole point of Paul's conviction is that eternal life has already begun through our baptism and faith because we are united to Jesus Christ. But death brings an intensification of life in Christ.

Paul exhorts the community of Philippi to live life with heaven as the horizon. 'Our citizenship is in heaven' (3:20) he writes. Use of the political image of citizenship would have appealed to the community of Philippi since it was a Roman colony.

Though Christians have not yet fully arrived in the new age that awaits them after death, they are already enrolled as citizens of heaven. In the one life we have we strive to grow more and more deeply in Christ. Then, in death, 'he will change our weak mortal bodies and make them like his own glorious body' (3:21).

Living in Christ

Paul sums up the Christian vision for his readers: For him, life is Christ (Phil 1:21). Everything else is 'rubbish' (3:8). Jesus

Christ is the 'living space', as it were, of the Christian community. And it is vital in the face of difficulties to recognise the importance of life in Christ.

Since they are already 'in Christ' and share in the Spirit they are to encourage one another (2:1). But, above all, Paul points again to the Cross of Christ and the power of the Resurrection. Every time we face difficulties, suffering, the Cross, if we imitate and share in Jesus' death, we can rise with him. Becoming like Jesus in his death, we can experience the power of his resurrection. Like a divine alchemy, we can pass from 'death' situations to 'life' (see 3:10-11; 4:11-13).

Of course, it is clear that Christians are only at the beginning of the Christian adventure that will culminate in physical death and resurrection. Paul talks of being on a race towards the goal. He indicates three important points for them to persevere in this race: forget the past, press onwards and keep one's eye on the goal (3:14). Eternal life will be the final outcome when, at the 'parousia', Christ will bring everything to completion.

Community life

Paul draws out the implications of 'being in Christ' for how the Philippians are to live as a community. He knows that there are divisions in the Christian community itself. As well as the outside criticisms, it seems that two women who held positions of prominence in the community are in conflict (4:2-3).

The community's capacity to stand firm in the face of difficulties, persecution and trials is weakened by internal divisions, self-seeking and pride. So Paul invites them to a new way of thinking. It's not enough just to have the heart, the will and the desire of Christ. They must put on the 'mind' of Christ and so be of 'one mind' and 'think one thing' in their relationships with one another (2:2).

And this is the heart of the lesson the Philippi community learned from Paul. If they want to influence the world about them, especially when there is a threat from outside the community (1:27-30), they must constantly mend the fabric of their own fellowship and life of communion (2:1-4). "Do nothing from selfishness or conceit, but in humility count others better than yourselves' (2:3).

The Christian attitude that builds community
Paul doesn't just recommend that the Christians get along together. He provides the model for how to achieve this. He does so in Phil 2:5-11, the most famous part of Paul's letter. By studying its rhythmic speech and transposing it into Aramaic, Scripture scholars believe this is a very early Christian hymn. It predates the letter.

The hymn tells of how Jesus Christ always enjoyed divine status; but, in the Incarnation, in becoming human, he 'emptied himself' of this divine status out of love for us. He even reached the point of dying on the cross for us. But God exalted Jesus to the highest place and gave him the name 'Lord' and transferred to the exalted Christ the universal eschatological homage given to God alone.

Apart from the enormous doctrinal contents in this hymn (it situates the 'story' of Jesus within the overall framework of God's eschatological plan to reclaim the universe for himself, seeing the historical selfless obedience in Jesus), Paul offers Jesus' 'self-emptying' as the model of Christian love. This is the 'attitude', the 'mind' they are to have in their own relationships with one another (2:5). The love Christ lived out *vis-à-vis* his Father and *vis-à-vis* us, we are now to live out *vis-à-vis* one another.

For Christians, 'to love' is to 'empty yourself' and to 'not be' out of love. If we live this mutually among one another, then we are imitating Jesus in his death and we are brought into the action of God who draws life out of death. When Christians love one another with the attitude of 'emptying' themselves (out of love), God who is Love conquers all and dwells among them. God himself is found in the unity and this conquers the opposition.

Daniel Harrington writes: 'This text indicates the extent to which Paul regarded the Gospel as something worth fighting for and how much he valued the union of hearts and minds within the Christian community.... What is at stake are the Philippians' identity as Christians and their manner of dealing with one another within the community of faith' (*Paul's Prison Letters*, New York: New City, 1997, p. 46).

Justification
In the context of the specific controversy over whether or not Christians should follow the practices such as circumcision and adhere in a certain way to the Law, Paul urges the members of the community of Philippi to be faithful to the Law-free gospel that he has preached.

Once again, Paul writes of his own experience. He had experienced a turnaround in his life at the time of his conversion and anything beyond knowing Christ at a deep personal level he now considers 'refuse'. 'For his sake I have suffered the loss of all things, and count them as refuse, in order that I may gain Christ and be found in him, not having a righteousness of my own, based on law, but that which is through faith in Christ, the righteousness from God that depends on faith' (3:9).

This is Paul's doctrine of justification. It's a theme Paul returns to frequently in his writings. He is convinced that believers have their righteousness 'from God'. What matters is that in eschewing all independent claims to right-standing, they allow themselves to be drawn in Christ into the sphere and scope of God's own righteousness' (2 Cor 5:21). So to know Christ and the power of his resurrection (Phil 3:10) is to experience him as 'life-giving Spirit' (1 Cor 15:45; 2 Cor 3:17), the one who conquers the forces of sin and death.

It is when we are weak that we experience his power. This was the paradox of Christianity that this early Christian community of Philippi was learning through facing their difficulties in the light of a deeper understanding of Jesus Christ.

5
The Christian Message Today

Trends in Christianity

Any attempt to trace trends and challenges in how Christianity interprets its message today has to take into account developments in the Church. And that is what this chapter sets out to do.

Throughout its history the Church and culture have been linked. After all, the people who make up the Church don't live out their faith in a vacuum. The huge cultural changes of recent times have also impacted on the Church. They are the context for understanding what the Holy Spirit 'is saying to the Church' (see Rev 2:7) at this moment of history.

In many ways the Church is going through a 'crisis'. Of course, a crisis is not necessarily a bad thing! People go through crises at different moments of their lives. Leaving childhood, becoming an adolescent, and entering the 'adult' world can be times of crisis. Likewise, a change of job, difficulties in a marriage relationship, or setbacks in the economy. But, in each case, the 'crisis' situation is ambiguous. It's not simply a topsy-turvy breakdown or collapse of things.

As we mentioned in chapter one, in the original sense of the Greek term, the word 'crisis' means a situation where things are hanging in the balance, where they are on a knife-edge. And this can either be positive or negative. In other words, a crisis situation is one in which old ways are coming to an end; but there's room for new possibilities.

A crisis situation presents itself as a challenge and a time for decision. And this is also the case for Christianity, the religion that has so marked Europe for the past two millennia.

The Church's history reminds us of various moments that were perceived as crises but which also resulted in new developments, clarifications and surprising outcomes: the tension over how Gentile Christians were to fit into the early Jewish-Christian communities; the changes involved in the rapid expansion of the Church from the fourth century onwards, when Christianity became the 'official' religion of the empire; the fourth-century disputes on the very nature of Jesus Christ; the collapse of the Roman Empire; the lay investiture controversy; the issue of simony; the Reformation; the collapse of the Papal states; the rise of Communism. An examination of the history of the Church in Ireland would also show a pattern of crisis and renewal (see Brendan Bradshaw and Dáire Keogh, *Christianity in Ireland: Revisiting the Story*, Dublin: Columba Press, 2002 and Patrick Corish, *The Irish Catholic Experience*, Dublin: Gill and Macmillan, 1985).

It's as if Jesus' death and resurrection that gave life to the Church continues to be the pattern of her constant renewal, development and new life.

A new stage along the Christian journey of faith
It is a curious feature that Christianity as a vibrant religious inspiration for people's everyday lives, culture and ethos, is diminishing in the Western world. How come this is occurring in the very region whose history has been so strongly Gospel-influenced?

In an insightful reading of the situation some years ago, Pope John Paul II commented that the crisis that the Church is experiencing today is not something coming in on us from outside Christianity. It's not simply a difficulty or some external obstacle in the work of evangelisation that has to be overcome. Rather, what we are going through is internal to Christianity. In order words, the difficulties encountered within Christianity today are to be viewed as a stage within the historical journey of the Christian faith. And the Pope offers a clue to what he believes is happening by pointing to the mystical experience of, for example, someone like St John of the Cross.

This Spanish mystic wrote of his spiritual experience as a follower of Jesus Christ. He went through what he described as a 'dark night' of faith where his belief in, as well as his understanding and knowledge of God were purified. The Pope compares the contemporary crisis that Christianity is going through with the phenomenon of a 'dark night' experienced in the spiritual life. Christian faith today is going through something like a spiritual dark night that has acquired an epochal dimension of collective proportions.

So Christianity is moving in a new direction. Christians are being invited to make a new and deeper discovery of God who is revealed to us in Jesus Christ. It's a time of new possibilities.

New times, new challenges
In many ways, the twenty-first century is calling Christians to be different from how they were before. Not that their essential doctrines are changeable, but rather certain aspects of the Gospel and new forms of Christian life need to emerge in a new and vibrant manner so that the Christian Message can be heard today.

For the Catholic Church, the Vatican Council was held precisely with this in mind. John XXIII, the Pope who called the Council, put it succinctly as follows: 'The substance of the ancient doctrine of the deposit of faith is one thing, and the way in which it is presented is another' (John XXIII, 'Opening Speech at Vatican II', in W. Abbott, ed., *The Documents of Vatican II*, Dublin: Geoffrey Chapman, 1967, p. 715).

It's not that Christianity needs to reinvent itself. More accurately, it could be claimed that Christianity today can really be more centred on its unique contribution as a religion of universal fraternity, mutual love, dialogue and peace among peoples. Circumstances point in this direction.

On the one hand, the world has become like a large city that is developing at an uncontrollable speed, advancing in all kinds of directions and with such a compulsion that humanity fears it is no longer free to decide its future on many issues.

On the other hand, the events of September 11th 2001, as well as new terrorist attacks such as those in Bali and Madrid, have led to a new and growing awareness of the need for humanity to find peaceful ways of co-existence, good government and a sense of direction so that the world-city can be a truly human space for the men, women and children who live there.

It is through these and many other circumstances that the Holy Spirit is opening the eyes of Christians to the importance of the Christian message for today's world and the need for Christians to give their contribution to a global situation crying out for a culture of interdependence between individuals, nations and peoples.

Paul Tillich, a twentieth-century theologian who advocated the correlation between religion and culture, spoke of theology needing to be an 'answering' theology, responding to the questions of our time (see *Systematic Theology* Vols I and II, Chicago, 1951 and 1957). Three challenges in particular call out for responses from Christianity today:

1. The challenge of what it means to be a *person* is a key contemporary issue at a time when the borderline and relationship between nature, technology and morality have become problematic. 'To be', 'can be' and 'ought to be' seem increasingly to be splitting apart. A new sense of personal and collective responsibility is needed in all areas

from bio-ethical questions to economics. This demands a renewed anthropology (an understanding of what it means to be human) that the Christian message needs to rediscover within itself and offer to the world.

Pope John Paul II is recognised the world over for his strong defence of the dignity of the human person and how this dignity needs to be respected in all walks of life, from the very beginnings of life to its natural end. A central element of his teaching is the belief that: 'In reality it is only in the mystery of the Word made flesh that the mystery of humanity truly becomes clear. For Adam, the first man, was a type of him who was to come, Christ the Lord. Christ the new Adam, in the very revelation of the mystery of the Father and of his love, fully reveals humanity to itself and brings to light its very high calling' (*Gaudium et Spes*, 22).

The Pope has also pointed to how natural science and Christian revelation are not in conflict. While each preserves its autonomy, both science and Christian faith can work together in the common quest for understanding the universe and the place of the human within it.

2. A second major challenge comes from the need to understand and handle the issue of *plurality and differences*. It is not uncommon now to hear people talk of a clash of civilisations (see Samuel P. Huntington, *The Clash of Civilizations and the Remaking of World Order*, New York: Touchstone, 1996). The issue of how to handle plurality and difference is to be found also at everyday levels in the arenas of thought, moral option, cultural encounter, religious affiliation, as well as the philosophy of human and social development.

Here again, Christians are rediscovering that their central doctrine, the Trinity, has something to say (*Catechism of the Catholic Church*, 234). The Christian God is a Community of Persons: Father, Son and Holy Spirit who love one another and who are One. There is unity in distinction in God and this is the foundation of, and model for, all unity in distinction within the world. It is this unity that Jesus brought on earth.

A very significant development in the context of the plurality of religions in the world has been the gathering of religious leaders together for prayer in initiatives promoted by the Catholic Church. Pope John Paul II initiated two such gatherings at a world level. They were held in Assisi in 1986 and 2002. In many ways these were 'icons' of the Second Vatican Council's definition of the Church as a sign and instrument of unity with God and the unity of humankind (see the document on the Church, *Lumen Gentium*, 1). In Dublin, on the initiative of Cardinal Connell, a gathering of religious leaders who made a commitment to peace took place in March 2002.

Christian Churches also participate in the World Conference of Religions for Peace. Churches and Church groups engage in numerous initiatives to foster healthy relationships between individuals, groups and peoples. See, for example, the Corrymeela community (www.corrymeela.org), or the Catholic Church's Pontifical Council for Justice and Peace www.vatican.va /roman_curia/pontifical_ councils/ justpeace).

3. *Globalisation*, or as some say 'Glocalisation', is a third key issue today that prompts a Christian response. There is a sense that, not just in economics but also in several other realms, the world is entering into a new era. It is increasingly becoming a multi-centred world with a world-perspective concerning the destiny of humanity.

Building up the world as one family resonates strongly with the mission of the Church. Already within the Church various voluntary agencies, new communities and movements as well as missionary orders and societies provide a spiritual network linking people across the globe. In various ways they contribute to giving a 'soul' to a world that has discovered its global technological unity but needs a spiritual 'soul' to give meaning to globalisation. The micro-experiences of the Church provide instances of local/global points of reference for a spiritual encounter between individuals and communities.

It is not surprising that, unlike previous Popes, John Paul II has travelled widely around the world emphasising the Church's unity. The World Youth Days held every few years have become global points of encounter between Christians. The Taizé gatherings have also underscored Christianity's contribution to a new multinational spiritual networking. In May 2004, many of the Catholic, Protestant and Orthodox movements and communities in Europe gathered together in Stuttgart for a celebration entitled 'Together for Europe'. Their desire was to render visible the spiritual network that already unites them in their contribution to building up a Europe of the spirit.

A spiritual turning point
The challenges just outlined could be summed up as the challenge of *meaning*, the challenge of the *other* and the challenge of the *one* (the one, not as uniformity downwards, but as a unity-symphony of diversity in the highest common denominator).

The message of Christianity today needs to be communicated as the Gospel of *meaning* in Jesus Christ (Lk 24:13-35), the Gospel of the *other* who is Jesus Christ (see Mt 25:31-46) and the Gospel of the *one,* Jesus Christ (Gal 3:28). Contemporary trends in Christianity are emerging along these lines.

Starting with a renewed recognition that God, in becoming flesh in his Son, definitively fulfilled the dignity and destiny of each individual, of the whole person and of all of humanity,

Christians today are being called to live out the Christian message focusing on the recognition of the triune God revealed in Jesus Christ as the horizon of freedom and truth and of plurality and unity. Within this perspective, while not imposing its view, Christianity offers the light of the Gospel to all arenas of life – from education to health, from politics to economics, from sport to music, from art to science, from migrant issues to justice, from ecology to communications.

A central aspect of the Gospel that has come to the fore is the recognition of 'the other', whoever he or she may be, as gift and possibility of a new future. Clearly, history tells us that the Christian religion hasn't always centred on this. No doubt, at a personal level, many Christians sought to do so – loving their neighbour, loving the poor. But today, Christians need to do so at the level of recognition of those who are culturally or religiously different. And this demands a deeper conversion to the Gospel of Jesus Christ.

That this is a time for new conversion is widely confirmed by many. The German theologian, Eugen Biser, for instance, contends that Christians have reached a new spiritual 'turning point' which opens up a new possibility for the Christian proclamation *(Glaubenswende: Eine Hoffnungsperspektive* (Herder, 1987, p. 115). He proposes two biblical icons that express key dimensions of the conversion needed for the Christian message to be heard again today. They express conversion to the 'mystical' depths of Christianity.

The first icon is that of Jesus Christ crucified who cries out in his abandonment on the cross. Our era has indeed been described as a 'landscape of the cry'. Biser remarks that: 'The cry – often fairly repressed – becomes a visible figure there where modern literature, philosophy, and psychology, as in particular in Karl Jaspers and Karl Gustav Jung, concentrate on the figure of Job and feel their problems are presented in this figure' (p. 113). Job's cry finds its echo and response in the cry of Christ on the Cross 'who, in his abandonment, not to be consoled by any visible help but only by addressing himself to God, gave to those who could not be helped in any manner other than that which only he could give: himself' (p. 67). The conversion here is to discover and hear Jesus' cry in all the suffering and questions of humanity.

The other biblical icon is that of the disciples on the road to Emmaus, of the disciples who discover the presence of the Lord in their midst, in that burning of their hearts, in their listening to the word and in the breaking of the Eucharistic bread, in which the risen Christ grasps and draws their existence towards its fullness. The conversion here is to the communitarian way of living our faith with Jesus present among us.

'Faith' – writes Biser – 'becomes perceptible there where preachers make the effort to translate the written testimonies into a living language. This takes place where, in the consciousness of the Christian community, those words are realised: "where two or three are gathered in my name, I am in the midst of them" (Mt 18:20)' (p. 75).

The philosopher Nietzsche spoke of needing to move into the adult age of faith. Perhaps it is with this in mind that Eugen Biser and others underline how Christian faith is about to enter into a new state of its existence, a mystical moment. In other words, it is primarily the *lived* experience of the Gospel and the intellectual insights emerging from this that will lead the Christian message to impact anew. As Biser writes, it is only a faith 'which is deepened from a mystical point of view which can reach humankind in its actual identity crisis and in its existential crisis' (p. 136).

Christianity in Ireland
The features we have been outlining above more generally hold true in the particular instance of Christianity in Ireland. While it is true, as the Anglican theologian, Andrew Pierce, has

perceptively commented, that Irish Christianity 'makes its presence felt ecclesiastically, much more so than philosophically or ideologically' (Dermot Lane, ed., *New Century, New Society*, Dublin: Columba Press, 1999, p. 12), the existential and mystical, intellectual and cultural rediscovery of central aspects of the Christian message will be crucial for the future of Christianity in Ireland.

It is not hard to agree that the biblical icon of the cry of Jesus on the Cross is one that sums up the cry of many who have felt betrayed, injured and confused by recent events in the Church. But likewise, the icon of the presence of Jesus in the midst of those gathered in his name indicates an ideal that attracts Irish people – community, fellowship, God not only in majesty beyond the stars but among us when we gather in his name.

Pierce rightly underlines a 'noticeable feature of the transitional situation of Irish Christianity', namely, 'that it has given rise to a question, not of Christianity *per se*, but of the churches and their behaviour'. Indeed 'it is important to acknowledge that... protests against the churches' actions and/or inactions do not necessarily call into question the coherence or credibility of Christianity as a worldview.'

The task facing Christianity in Ireland is to re-present the vision, the ideal, and the excitement of Jesus Christ in credible models to people who are searching.

Christianity and dialogue

Following on from what we've been saying above, there is one word that guides the Church of Christ at this time of history in its desire to represent the message of Christianity. And that word is 'dialogue'. In 1964, Paul VI in *Ecclesiam Suam* pointed out that the attitude the Catholic Church has to take on in this hour of history is that of dialogue: 'The Church must enter into dialogue with the world in which it lives. It has something to say, a message to give, a communication to make' (*Ecclesiam Suam*, 65).

It was a spirit of dialogue that led Pope John XXIII to call the Second Vatican Council, the single biggest event that is still the main inspiration for the Catholic Church. It was the spirit of dialogue that prompted John Paul II to call leaders of the world's religions together for the two Assisi meetings for peace in 1986 and 2002. It is the spirit of dialogue that lies behind countless initiatives of the Church in furthering peace, social justice, health care, education and the contact with the arts. The spirit of dialogue was the inspiring spark that brought to life the World Council of Churches and its outreach to civil society (see Konrad Raiser, *To be the Church*, Geneva: WCC Publications, 1997).

It is important to note that dialogue is not a tactic adopted from 'outside' the Church but rather a rediscovery of the very form of revelation itself (see the Vatican II documents, *Dei Verbum* and *Dignitatis humanae*). God's self-communication took place in a dialogue made up of words and deeds with humanity, a dialogue that culminated in *The* Word become flesh: Jesus Christ.

Several Gospel and New Testament episodes indicate the way of dialogue: the conversation between Jesus and his disciples (Mk 8), between Jesus and the woman of Samaria (Jn 4), between Paul and the philosophers in Athens (Acts 17:16-34).

The Church has its origins in dialogue
As we've just mentioned, God's self-communication to humanity took the form of a dialogue of words and deeds that culminated in Jesus. It was through his life, death and resurrection that the Church came to life. And, through the Church, he continues to dialogue with us.

In the power of the Holy Spirit, the Risen Christ continues to be present and carries on his mission of building up the Church through the authoritative preaching of the faith and the celebration of the seven sacraments. In its sacramental and hierarchical essence, the Church cannot be altered.

The Eucharist and the other sacraments are guaranteed points of encounter with the Risen Jesus Christ who comes to meet us in his concrete, visible and tangible signs of love. In the sacramental encounters, through the action of the Holy Spirit, the Risen Jesus Christ draws us into a new life in the heart of God the Father who is love (1 Jn 4:8, 16). This life is an anticipation of the salvation that will blossom fully in heaven. It really does begin already here on earth, if we are open to receiving the gift of grace.

- In baptism we are received into the family of the Church.
- Confirmation strengthens us as witnesses of Christ.
- In the sacrament of reconciliation, through the ministry of the Church, Christ forgives us and cancels out our sins seventy times seven.
- Through the Eucharist the Church nourishes us with the Body of Christ.
- The love between two spouses is sealed in a divine way in the sacrament of marriage.
- The sacrament of Holy Orders gives us bishops and priests who are ordained instruments of the Risen Christ teaching, sanctifying and guiding the Church.
- And, finally, in the sacrament of the Anointing of the Sick, the Church accompanies those who are ill and, together with the Eucharist, sets those in their last moments of life on the pathway to God.

So the Church always has its origins in Jesus Christ. We could never be Church if he did not build us up as Church. But the Church is not an end in itself! Christ builds us up so that we can continue his presence and mission in the world. Through us God continues to dialogue with humanity.

As the people of God and the Body of Christ, the Church's whole mission is to go outside herself to give witness to and proclaim the Gospel. We are built up as the Body of Christ by the Risen Christ through the preaching of the faith and the sacraments, so that all of us together continue his mission of teaching, sanctifying and building community in the world.

The Church is communion (Koinōnia)
While the sacramental and hierarchical essence of the Church cannot change, the everyday expression of the Church varies in each generation. And it is at this level, in the words of the German pastor and martyr, Dietrich Bonhoeffer, that we need to 'recast the form of the Church'.

It is the recasting of the Church for our time that has been going on throughout all the Churches in recent times. We see it at the Catholic Church's Vatican Council, at the World Council of Churches' Assemblies, at the Anglican Communion's Lambeth Conferences.

The guiding notion in this recasting is *koinōnia*, a word that means 'communion' or 'fellowship'. This is directly linked to the focus on dialogue that we have just seen above. To say the Church is a community or fellowship is to say that the Church is a people gathered into unity, participating in and modelled on the supreme dialogue of love between God the Father, Son and Holy Spirit.

This guiding notion acts as a corrective to two extreme tendencies that are sometimes found among Christians. On the one hand, some live their Christian faith in a very individual-centred way without any real experience of the Church-community. On the other hand some live their faith with a self-satisfied or reactionary centring on their own Church, excluding others.

The Christianity Jesus Christ wants receives its true form from the Gospel and from the breath of the Spirit. And both the Gospel and the Spirit point away from the extremes of individualism and ecclesiocentrism.

The focus on communion, however, demands of all a conversion both in the way of looking at things and in the way of going about things.

The recasting of the spirit and style of Church life has, of course, to impact on institutional and organisation levels. But it would be a false reform – as the Dominican theologian, Yves Congar, once wrote – if the reform did not start from the heart and follow ways indicated by the breath of the Spirit. Yes, we need to recast the visible face of the Church, but a face-lift is not enough!

To build up the Church as Communion is to dig deep and rediscover we are brothers and sisters united in the name of Jesus Christ and live together a daily dialogue of life based on the Gospel.

Structures and a spirituality of communion
Within the Catholic Church there has been quite a development in recent years in the attempt to recast the shape of the Church as communion. New or renewed structures of participation have emerged such as synods, pastoral councils and parish councils.

Lay people, both men and women, now speak at the synods of bishops and at local synods. They become members of pontifical and diocesan councils and commissions, committees and agencies. Many lay people study theology. There is greater recognition of the variety of ministries of lay people within the Church. Greater attention is given to how lay people live out their baptismal calling to holiness in their families, their work place and their many activities in social and political, cultural and recreational pursuits.

Above all, however, the drive to build up the Church as communion is leading everyone to work for a Church that is more a home and not simply an 'ecclesiastical organisation'.

A vibrant phenomenon in this regard is the emergence of new ecclesial movements such as L'Arche (www.larche.ie), Focolare (www.focolare.ie), and Sant'Egidio (www.santegidio.org). Well over fifty of these groups have come to life in the past fifty years, providing new community forms of encounter with the Gospel for millions of Catholics worldwide. These communities aren't just made up of lay people. Bishops, priests and religious as well as married people, young people and old people, all come together in these communities within the Big Community, the Church.

Each of these new movements or communities seems to embody a particular aspect of Gospel spirituality. Often their outreach goes beyond the Catholic Church to members of other Churches, other faiths and people of non-religious convictions. Of particular note is a strong focus on a communitarian spirituality found in these new movements and communities.

The issue of spirituality is, of course, gaining a new prominence throughout the Church. Indeed, many commentators note how contemporary Christian spirituality reveals new emerging trends in Christianity.

There's a focus on a lived, mystical experience of God. The link between spirituality and concrete, social and political commitment is greater. Walter Kasper points to a deeper concentration on essential elements of Christian devotion and faith today. There's a new and enthusiastic sense of Church as a living community. An increasing feature in Christian spirituality today is an outreach to the experience of other Christian Churches and other religions. An inculturated spirituality is in vogue. Holistic concerns are viewed as important. There's greater attention to the feminine and women's experience.

Echoing many of these trends and commenting on the direction of the Church at the beginning of the new millennium, Pope John Paul II has written that 'we need *to promote a spirituality of communion,* making it the guiding principle... Let us have no illusions: unless we follow this spiritual path, external structures of communion will serve very little purpose. They would become mechanisms without a soul, "masks" of communion rather than its means of expression and growth' (*Novo Millennio Ineunte,* 43). He is convinced that Christians need to supply 'institutional reality with a soul' (45).

This 'soul' comes from the Gospel rediscovered. As Pope Paul VI wrote in the 1975 encyclical *Evangelii nuntiandi*, 19: The Gospel has the power to change our 'criteria of judgment, determining values, points of interest, lines of thought, sources of inspiration and models of life'.

The search for Christian unity

The scandal of Christian division demands dialogue among Christians and among the Churches. There is but one Church of Jesus Christ. And yet, taking the Gospel scene where Jesus invites people to 'come and see' (Jn 2:1:35-39) as typical of Christianity's way of evangelisation, Christians have to admit that they confuse people because of the conflicting addresses they give of where they live! Division among Christians takes greatly from the credibility of the Church's preaching of Jesus Christ.

There are four major moments of division in Christian history. The first arose in the context of what are called the Christological controversies in the fourth and fifth centuries. The Ancient Churches of the East (often called the Oriental Orthodox churches) such as the Syrian Orthodox, Coptic, Armenian, Assyrian and Ethiopian Orthodox Churches are linked to this era.

1054 is a date associated with the division between the Eastern and Western 'lungs' of Christianity. This came about through a combination of cultural, political and social factors going right back to tensions between the Latin West and Byzantine East of the Roman Empire. Different approaches to liturgy, spirituality, theology, church structure and relationships to the state also led to a gradual alienation of East and West. While many dates could be used to symbolise the split, the one most commonly used is 1054 because in that year Cardinal Humbert excommunicated the Patriarch Cerularius in the basilica of Hagia Sophia in Constantinople (modern day

Istanbul). One of the areas that continues to be of theological concern to the Eastern Orthodox is the insertion by Latin Christians of the phrase 'and the Son' into the Creed in speaking of the Holy Spirit's procession within the Trinity. The Eastern Orthodox churches include the Greek Orthodox, the Russian Orthodox, the Rumanian Orthodox, the Serbian Orthodox and the Bulgarian Orthodox churches.

The Continental Reformation that occurred in Western Europe began with Martin Luther (1483-1546) in 1517. The Reformation focus is sometimes summed up as *scripture alone, faith alone, grace alone*. It emphasised the priesthood of all believers and the doctrine of justification. From Luther came the Evangelical Lutheran churches of Germany and Scandinavia.

Other major figures in the Continental Reformation include the Swiss Reformers John Calvin of Geneva (1509-1564) and Ulrich Zwingli of Zurich (1484-1531). From them came the churches called 'Reformed' and include (through the influence of John Knox and also the Puritan revolution in England) the Scottish Presbyterian and the Irish Presbyterian Churches.

The Anglican Communion is linked with the English Reformation that originated with Henry VIII (1509-1547). It considers itself Reformed and Catholic. A large number of Churches belong to the worldwide Anglican Communion, including the Church of Ireland.

Subsequent developments in Europe, America and Africa led to the evolution of other Churches. In the seventeenth century the Baptist movement and the Religious Society of Friends (Quakers) emerged. In the eighteenth century the revival within Protestant Churches led eventually in England, for instance, to the evolution of a separate Church after John Wesley's (1702-1791) death, called the Methodist Church (1784). In the nineteenth century urgency about the second coming of Christ at the end of time produced a variety of movements that developed into Churches such as the Seventh-day Adventists.

A Pentecostal revival movement based on the Holiness movement, a Wesleyan emphasis on experience, the Holy Spirit and a second work of grace, started in Los Angeles, California, in 1906 and was soon to develop into one of the fastest growing Christian communities in the late twentieth century. It has resulted in various Churches coming to life such as the Assemblies of God and Church of God in Christ. A Pentecostal spirit is also to be found in minority ethnic churches such as the black majority churches that have sprung up in Africa in the twentieth century.

Prompted by the Word of God and the action of the Holy Spirit, all Churches, to greater or lesser degrees, have committed themselves to a new drive to correspond to Jesus' last will and testament: 'may they all be one' (Jn 17:21). In his encyclical on ecumenism, John Paul II comments on the meaning of Jesus' prayer for unity as follows: 'to believe in Christ means to desire unity; to desire unity means to desire the Church; to desire the Church means to desire the communion of grace which corresponds to the Father's plan from all eternity. Such is the meaning of Christ's prayer' (*Ut Unum Sint*, 9).

The twentieth century saw an enormous development in relationships between the Churches. The 1910 Missionary Conference held in Edinburgh is normally viewed as the birthday of the Ecumenical Movement. Since then an unimaginable progress has been made. It is difficult for those born more recently to appreciate the degree of this progress. It has been a time when Christians of various Churches have discovered themselves as baptised brothers and sisters in the one Church of Christ.

At Vatican II, the Catholic Church committed herself to work for Christian unity. The Church sees this unity as confession of one faith, the common celebration of divine worship and the fraternal harmony of the family of God. Along with many others, the Catholic Church believes that the goal of the ecumenical movement is the full visible communion of all

Christians. Unity, of course, does not mean uniformity. There can be a variety of expressions but a unity in the essential faith, worship and communion of life of the Church.

Achievements

Ecumenical activity takes place at many levels, at a parish level, at the level of associations, movements, communities and religious orders, as well as at a national level and at a global level. It has many dimensions – the dialogue of charity, the dialogue of doctrine, the dialogue of experience, the dialogue of life, the dialogue of prayer.

At present, the Catholic Church has a council in Rome dedicated exclusively to ecumenical dialogue. On a world level, the Catholic Church engages in fourteen bi-lateral dialogues. On a local level, each diocese has an ecumenical officer and often an ecumenical commission or committee. Episcopal conferences around the world engage in dialogues with the Churches in their region.

The Anglican Communion is engaged in many dialogues and each national Church is actively committed to furthering bi-lateral and multi-lateral dialogues. In 1996, for instance, the Anglican Churches of Scotland, Wales, England and Ireland signed an agreement of full communion with the Lutheran Churches of Scandinavia and the Baltics. It is known as the Porvoo Declaration.

The 'official' dialogues have made great headway. Major documents have been published indicating mutual understanding, new directions for the future and breakthroughs in theologically difficult points of disagreement between the Churches.

In 1982, for instance, the Faith and Order commission of the World Council of Churches published the 'Lima document', a discussion document on Baptism, Eucharist and Ministry (BEM). It has become a very positive springboard for further theological reflection. Other significant developments within the Ecumenical

Movement include the dialogue carried on by the Anglican-Roman Catholic International Commission (ARCIC), the 1999 joint Lutheran-Roman Catholic *Joint Declaration on Justification* (a key Reformation issue) and recent agreed statements on doctrine between the Catholic Church and some of the Ancient Eastern Churches. The World Alliance of Reformed Churches and the World Methodist Council have also engaged in numerous dialogues both with the Catholic Church and other Churches.

Church leaders from different denominations now meet regularly together to share news, review developments, pray together and work on common issues. In April 2001 the Conference of European Churches and the Council of European Bishops' Conferences signed an ecumenical charter called *Charta Oecumenica* outlining guidelines for the growing cooperation among the Churches in Europe.

It is not uncommon for ministers of different Churches to be invited to other Churches to pass on greetings or attend liturgies. Chaplains of different denominations work side by side in hospitals and colleges.

In the area of mixed marriages, the issue of the Catholic partner having to sign a promise to bring up children as Catholic has been removed. Now what the Catholic partner signs is a commitment to do what he or she can, within the unity of the partnership of marriage, to have the children baptised and brought up in the Catholic faith.

At the level of the dialogue of experience and prayer, there are many ecumenical initiatives promoted by religious orders, organisations, movements and communities. Ecumenical formation and projects are also carried out as part of the religious education in school programmes and theological institutes.

Difficulties
Despite promising developments, there are still difficulties. Issues of doctrinal differences remain in areas such as the

relationship of Scripture and Tradition, the Eucharist, Ordination as a Sacrament, the Magisterium of the Church (especially the role of the Pope) and Mary.

It is important, of course, to remember that what unites Christians is much more than what divides them. So, even within the broad areas of disagreement, there are many elements where there is agreement. So, it is necessary to avoid simplistic statements like 'Roman Catholics and the Orthodox Churches believe in Mary and Protestants do not'!

Apart from doctrinal difficulties with concrete implications, as in the case of sharing in sacramental liturgical worship, especially the Eucharist, other issues arise that are painful for all the Churches.

Impatience at the slow progress can lead to tensions. Clearly, the urgency that many Christians sense is a good thing. It indicates the clear will of God that Christians be united. But at times the sense of urgency can risk wanting to reach the goal without taking the steps necessary to reach that goal. The developments at the official levels of dialogue need time to be 'owned' and 'received' by all the people of God so that a healthy ecumenism prevails.

At a time when the issue of truth-claims is controversial in Western culture in general, there is a risk that relativism enters into Christianity under the guise of ecumenical dialogue. This can be a difficulty. It is relativism or a false irenicism more than ecumenism to say the differences don't matter at all, so let's just forget about them as if they don't exist.

A healthy ecumenism involves also the pain of searching for the way forward together. It is based on Jesus Christ who said of himself: 'I am the Truth' (Jn 14:6). True ecumenism and healthy inter-Church relations aim at unity in the truth and not at the expense of it. Ecumenism is a prophetic action and never a compromise.

The socio-political context can often be a difficulty in ecumenical dialogue. Partners to the dialogue carry the baggage of history and culture that makes the reconciling of memory, healing and forgiveness more complicated. Prejudices and fears are not easy to overcome. Dealing with the past is not easy (see David Stevens, 'Dealing with the past', *The Furrow*, 55 (2004), pp. 148-155).

Dialogue of life
It is clear that there is a need for a 'dialogue of life' among Christians and Churches. They have lived apart for several centuries, developing different practices, praying in different ways, approaching the Gospel from different perspectives. The 'dialogue of life' involves Christians increasingly sharing what they have in common with one another and trying to live that together: the Scriptures, the Creeds, several of the early Councils, the life of grace, some of the sacraments, charisms and spirituality.

Commenting on what the future might be like, Cecily Boland summarises the Catholic belief 'that the one Church will not be a repetition of past structural uniformity, but a communion which embraces all the gifts of the Spirit present in other Christian churches and ecclesial communities.... On the way to that goal of full visible communion, Catholics should, after the example of the Pope, look for and encourage opportunities and means of living out in practice the degree of imperfect communion that we already recognise' (Paul Avis, ed., *The Church: An Introduction to the Major Traditions*, London: SPCK, 2002, pp. 102-103).

Christian faith ultimately is not a question of claims and counter-claims. It cannot be announced without witnessing or without martyrdom. If Christ said he is the truth he showed it when he gave himself right to the point of abandonment on the wood of the cross.

Jesus Christ gave himself and emptied himself for us. In Jesus we see that God goes outside himself and reaches us where we are. Christian faith and witness to the truth are communicated only in the self-giving and martyrdom modelled on Jesus Christ. 'To love truth – wrote Simon Weil – means to put up with the emptiness and so to accept death. Truth is on the side of death', meaning that dying to ourselves is necessary in all search for truth; and that sentiment is also true in ecumenism.

Ecumenism in Ireland
Prior to the 1960s the Protestant and Catholic worlds on the island of Ireland were very self-contained with very little interaction between them. But the 1960s brought a change in Irish society, both North and South, and also in terms of relationships among Christians (see Ian Ellis, *Vision and Reality: A Survey of Twentieth Century Irish Inter-Church Relations*, Belfast, Queen's University, 1992, and Michael Hurley, *Christian Unity: An Ecumenical Second Spring*, Dublin: Veritas, 1998).

On the one hand, it can be said that relationships have been transformed over the past forty years, particularly at Church leadership level. The degree of meetings, co-operation and interaction would have been unimaginable forty years ago.

The main official ecumenical meeting point in Ireland is The Irish Inter-Church Meeting (see www.irishchurches.org), which first took place at Ballymascanlon in September 1973. Since 1984 the Inter-Church Committee, made up of leaders and representatives of the members of the Irish Council of Churches and of the Episcopal Conference of the Roman Catholic Church, meets several times a year.

The Irish Council of Churches is constituted by the following member Churches: The Cherubim and Seraphim Church in Ireland; The Church of Ireland; The Coptic Orthodox Church in Ireland; The Greek Orthodox Church in Britain and Ireland; The Life Link Network of Churches; The Lutheran Church in Ireland; The Methodist Church in Ireland; The Irish District of the Moravian Church; The Non-Subscribing Presbyterian Church of Ireland; The Presbyterian

Church in Ireland; The Salvation Army (Ireland Division); The Religious Society of Friends in Ireland; The Russian Orthodox Church in Ireland; The Romanian Church in Ireland.

There are many encouraging inter-Church initiatives in Ireland. Services during the Week of Prayer for Christian Unity are now commonplace. The Annual Women's World Day of Prayer has increasingly seen women of various denominations come together. Groups engage together in bible studies and discussion of Church documents. Concrete projects become occasions for cooperation and friendship such as those initiatives fostering education for mutual understanding, joint study of local history, the organising of conferences, and concrete social initiatives. Christmas carol services and other annual events are sometimes held jointly.

There have been a number of pioneers of Irish ecumenism. Among many others, recent publications bring the names of the Jesuit priest, Michael Hurley, and the Methodist minister, Eric Gallagher, to mind (see Michael Hurley, *Christian Unity: An Ecumenical Second Spring*, Dublin: Veritas, 1998, and Dennis Cooke, *Peacemaker: the life and work of Eric Gallagher*, Methodist Publishing House, 2004).

Noteworthy initiatives in Irish ecumenism have been the annual Glenstal Ecumenical Conference, held since 1964, and the Greenhills Conference (near Drogheda), which began in 1966. A major milestone was the inauguration of The Irish School of Ecumenics in 1970 (www.tcd.ie/ise). Since 2001 Edgehill Methodist College, Belfast and Mater Dei Institute, Dublin, jointly teach an undergraduate degree in theology. The charismatic movement has also featured in the history of Irish ecumenism. The work of the Ecumenical Society of the Blessed Virgin Mary and the Legion of Mary also deserve mention. An important step in Irish Ecumenism took place in September 2002, when the Methodist Church in Ireland and the Church of Ireland signed a covenant acknowledging what both Churches hold in common and undertaking 'to share a common life and mission' and 'to grow together so that unity may be visibly realised.'

Northern Ireland
Despite moments of darkness, there has been a significant range of initiatives in inter-Church relations in Northern Ireland (see Eric Gallagher & Stanley Worrall, *Christians in Ulster: 1968-1980*, Oxford University Press, 1982). It would be well nigh impossible to calculate the considerable numbers of seeds of reconciliation and dialogue sown by countless individuals and communities in the past forty years. There can be no doubt that very many of the cross-community projects are Christian inspired (see www.communityrelations.org.uk).

Inter-Church groups, Church forums, education for peace projects, and fellowship meals are increasing in Northern Ireland. One of the more prominent initiatives is the Clonard/Fitzroy Fellowship which promotes contact, mutual understanding, respect and common witness between people from the various Christian traditions in Northern Ireland, beginning with the Presbyterian congregation at Fitzroy and the Roman Catholic congregation at Clonard. It was awarded the Pax Christi International Peace Prize in 1999.

Disturbed by the brokenness of God's people in Northern Ireland, and urged on by a common love of the Lord Jesus, the group began in 1981 as an inter-Church Bible study group set up under the inspiration of the late Fr Christopher McCarthy of Clonard Monastery and Rev. Ken Newell, Minister at Fitzroy Presbyterian Church. The fellowship group meets each month alternately in Fitzroy and Clonard.

While retaining its initial bible study and prayer focus, the group has developed and has become a dialogue forum for an exchange of life, news, traditions and spiritual experience. It's a forum where members can gradually learn more about each other's traditions. It organises various activities including

Reconciliation Services for large congregations of the Church at both Fitzroy and Clonard. The fellowship group wants to be a sign of unity within a divided Church.

One of the fellowship's aims is to develop an ongoing dialogue with members of groups involved in the cultural and political life of Northern Ireland, e.g. Nationalist and Unionist politicians, members of the Loyal Orders, GAA, and so on. In 2004 a series of meetings addressed the issue of racism in Northern Ireland.

Difficulties and new challenges in Ireland
The cultural and historical context plays an important role in the relations between Christians of different Churches on this island. Violence and sectarianism have led to deep prejudices, hurt and painful memories that can easily block engagement in any outreach to or dialogue with members of another tradition. Indeed, the very word 'ecumenism' is off-putting for some with 'inter-Church relations' a preferred term. The Partners in Transformation Project that we'll look at below is discovering the depth of imbedded attitudes.

The biggest challenge is, in fact, as elsewhere, the 'reception' of ecumenical and inter-Church developments of 'mainstream' ecumenism/inter-Church relations among all members of the Church. In other words, the challenge facing all the Churches is how the developments in the official ecumenical dialogues are being communicated and taken on board by all members of the Church. It's a time to rediscover what the ecumenical movement seeks to achieve.

A difficulty also exists in relation to the issue of sharing in sacramental liturgical worship, especially the Eucharist. The Churches have not yet reached full doctrinal communion on this issue and its associated doctrinal aspects. It is a very delicate area also because it is read through the prism of our recent history of the 'troubles' between the divided communities in Northern Ireland. Nevertheless, here too, to go straight to the goal without passing through the steps on the way to that goal could end up doing more harm than good.

There are two principles that govern the Catholic Church's approach to the issue of sacramental liturgical worship. Firstly, Catholics understand the Church as a sacrament of Christ's presence in the world and that individual sacraments take place in a concrete community as the sign of the reality of its unity in faith, worship and community life. From the point of view of the Eucharist as a sign of unity, the Church's position is that accession to the Eucharist is appropriate to those who share in oneness in faith, worship and ecclesial life. This principle would stress the reason why there cannot be open sacramental liturgical worship where members of other Churches would receive communion in the Catholic Church.

A second principle the Catholic Church follows in this area is the recognition that the sacraments build the unity of the Church and nourish us. So, from the point of view of the Eucharist as a grace and means of building the Church, access to the Eucharist may be permitted, or even commended, for Christians of other Churches and ecclesial communities. In other words this principle would stress the reason why there can be open sacramental liturgical worship where members of other Churches can receive communion in the Catholic Church.

Following on from these principles, at present, Christians of other Churches are permitted to receive communion in the Catholic Church only in special circumstances to meet a grave spiritual need. Of course, to receive communion presupposes the member of the other Church freely requests this and has Catholic faith in the Eucharist.

In Ireland, the fact of two jurisdictions impinges on ecumenical dialogue. On the one hand, the search for unity among the Churches helps keep alive the sense of all of us living on one and the same island. But the different 'worlds' can lead to different expectations, practices and experiences of inter-Church relations on the island of Ireland.

A major shift in ecumenism is coming about with the growth of Orthodox Churches, minority ethnic Churches and new Churches in Ireland. The new developments will alter considerably the ecumenical landscape and this can only have repercussions on inter-Church relations.

Since 1996 up to 200,000 foreign immigrants have come into the Republic of Ireland, comprising 5 per cent of the population. The Orthodox presence increased from 358 in 1991 to 10,437 in 2002. Many Black Majority Churches have been established and are developing at a fast rate all over the country. It is reckoned there could be up to 10,000 people in these Churches.

Other faith communities are also growing; and this too impacts on ecumenical relations, as it invites Christians to reflect on their common witness and openness to other faith communities. The 2002 Census gave the number of Muslims in the Republic of Ireland as 19,100, up from 3,900 in 1991. The Jewish Community now numbers 1,790, up from 1,581 in 1991. The Buddhist Community has reached 3,894, up from 986. The Hindu Community is now 3,099, up from 953.

New issues are also coming to the fore in the ecumenical agenda. There is an increasing diversity within mainline traditions concerning issues such as gay lifestyles and abortion.

Moving beyond sectarianism

Sectarianism has received considerable attention in Ireland, especially since the Good Friday Belfast Agreement. It has been defined as a system 'of attitudes, actions, beliefs and structures at personal, communal, and institutional levels which always involves religion, and typically involves a negative mixing of religion and politics... which arises as a distorted expression of positive, human needs especially for belonging, identity and the free expression of difference... and is expressed in destructive patterns of relating' (Joseph Liechty and Cecelia Clegg, (eds.), *Moving Beyond Sectarianism*, Dublin: Columba, 2001, pp. 102-103).

All ecumenical initiatives are in some way linked to the attempt to move beyond sectarianism. As the Vatican II document on ecumenism (a document always relevant and worth re-reading) puts it: 'The term "ecumenical movement" indicates the initiatives and activities encouraged and organized... to promote Christianity unity. These are: first, every effort to avoid expressions, judgments and actions which are not truthful and fair in representing the situation of the members of the separated Christian communities.... (*Unitatis Redintegratio*, 4).

Various bodies have endeavoured to create a culture that moves beyond sectarianism. We've already pointed to the Fitzroy/Clonard initiative between congregations of the Roman Catholic Church and the Presbyterian Church. We shall now list a few major initiatives in which all the mainline Churches are involved.

The Irish Council of Churches and the Roman Catholic Church's Irish Commission for Justice and Peace have co-operated in *The Churches' Peace Education Programme*. This programme aims to produce educational materials for use in schools, Churches and other groups. It works with teachers, Church educators and others to promote education for mutual understanding. It also promotes and disseminates resources. Their catalogue is available from the Columba Centre, St Patrick's College, Maynooth, Co. Kildare.

A major initiative in combatting sectarianism was a six-year research project carried out by Joseph Liechty and Cecelia Clegg of the Irish School of Ecumenics. All the mainline Churches contributed. The results of this work have been published in the *Moving Beyond Sectarianism* book cited above.

The project sought to examine the role of Christian religion in sectarianism in Northern Ireland. It did so through group work aimed at helping groups from neighbouring Protestant and Catholic parishes, clergy forums, community relations and reconciliation organisations, grassroots inter-Church initiatives and others, to address the problem of sectarianism. It also involved interviewing a wide range of people to gather insights into their experiences of sectarianism and reconciliation.

On the basis of their complex process of consultation, the researchers then set about disseminating the results of their findings; running training events to pass on skills and knowledge necessary to address sectarianism; organising and leading a Church consultation designed to help the Churches move forward in the ways that they challenge sectarianism; and publishing their findings. Arising from this project, some accessible materials were developed by the Irish School of Ecumenics for use in a range of key sectors.

Following on from this project, a joint initiative was launched in 2001 by the Irish School of Ecumenics and Mediation Northern Ireland. The *Partners in Transformation* project seeks to promote active peace-building as a mainstream concern and not the preserve of an enthusiastic few within the the Churches. One of its aims is to map the peace-building initiatives currently taking place and the training being provided in each denomination or faith community, to build up an accurate picture of what is happening and the gaps that exist.

By way of conclusion to this subsection it is necessary to note also the work of the Evangelical Contribution on Northern Ireland (ECONI). It sets out to reflect critically on the identity of evangelical Protestantism in Northern Ireland (www.econi.org). Another new initiative is the *Churches Together of Britain and Ireland* initiative called *Building Bridges Together* (www.geocities.com/ccom_ctbi/Building_Bridges_of_Hope.html)

Ireland and the bigger search for unity
It is always necessary to remember that inter-Church relations in Ireland are part of a larger story, the great ecumenical story throughout the whole Church worldwide.

Many Churches in Ireland work together in *The Churches Together of Britain and Ireland* (www.ctbi.org.uk). It's an umbrella body that covers things it makes sense to do in common across more than one of the nations that make up Britain and Ireland.

Currently, the Methodist Church in Ireland and the Church of Ireland are full members while the Roman Catholic Episcopal Conference in Ireland is an associate member. Mrs Gillian Kingston of the Methodist Church in Ireland is one of the moderators of the Churches Representatives Meetings of the CTBI.

The Methodist Church and the Church of Ireland are members of the World Council of Churches (WCC). The Catholic Church works closely with the WCC. The Presbyterian Church withdrew from the WCC in 1980.

The Roman Catholic Episcopal Conference in Ireland is linked with the Pontifical Council for the Promotion of Christian Unity in Rome. Currently, Bishop Anthony Farquhar, Auxiliary Bishop of Down and Connor, is chairman of the international Roman Catholic – World Alliance of Reformed Churches' dialogue.

Interpreting the message, incarnating the Gospel
So far we have reviewed the Church's own internal movement towards greater communion and also the Church's ecumenical movement. It is a major contemporary trend. The Church sees herself as carrying on the mission of Jesus but always needing to be reformed so that she can in turn interpret the message for the world around her.

However, for the past one hundred years, there has been an increased attention across all the Churches to the social and cultural implications of Christian faith. The Church looks to humanity in a spirit of service and concrete love. It seeks to carry on the mission of Jesus who came 'to serve and not to be served'. There has been a renewed commitment on the part of the Church to seeing and loving concretely the face of Jesus in all the divisions, suffering and hardship in the world. As Pascal put it: Christ is crying out until the end of the world. He took on all the wounds of humanity, so the Church must love him in situations of conflict, injustice, suffering and loneliness.

Within the Catholic Church, for instance, a whole body of social teaching has come to light. To communicate this teaching is seen as an integral part of proclaiming Jesus Christ, who redeemed humanity and the relationships between people. The Christian faith is neither a private devotion nor a fleeing from the world. There is a new sense within Christianity that the grammar of relationship is essential in experiencing both who God is and what it is to be human, since we have been created in the image and likeness of God. But our social teaching has to become concrete. The Gospel has to be incarnated.

Carrying on the mission of Jesus: Church structures and authority
For the Church to be able to give and continue Jesus' mission, she has to *be*! In other words, the Church is a social-corporate-visible reality in the world. Just as one's skeleton is essential to one's body, likewise the Church's structures are vital to the life of the Body of Christ.

Admittedly, it's not the skeleton that we see first when we meet a person. Likewise, the visible structures are not the most important feature that we need to focus on when reflecting on the Church. But they are vital to the effectiveness of the Church carrying on the mission of Jesus.

While there are always grounds for a critique of 'institutionalism' in the Church (an exaggerated or rigid clinging to all historical forms of Church organisation), it would be a naïve vision of things to say the Church's institution is bad. The sacraments and the hierarchical structure of the Church are essential institutional elements without which the Church would flounder. Within the Catholic Church, the words of Jesus to Peter 'You are Peter and on this rock I will build my community' (Mt 16:18) are interpreted as pointing to the concrete, institutional dimension of the Church as willed by Jesus Christ.

Each Church is organised in its own particular way. Paul Avis has edited a work that provides an overview of the Orthodox Churches, the Reformed Churches, the Methodist Churches, the Roman Catholic Church, the Baptist and Pentecostal Churches, the Churches of the Anglican Communion, the Old Catholic Churches of the Union of Utrecht and the Lutheran Churches (see Paul Avis, ed., *The Christian Church: An Introduction to the Major Traditions*, London: SPCK, 2002).

Good summaries of the nature and exercise of authority in the Anglican Communion and the Roman Catholic Church are to be found in the 1999 Agreed Statement of the Anglican-Roman Catholic International Commission (ARCIC), *The Gift of Authority: Authority in the Church III* (London: CTS, 1999).

The Catholic Church's structures and authority
A consideration of structures and authority within the Catholic Church would require a lengthy treatment. For a start, it must be remembered that while most of us belong to what is called the Latin rite of the Catholic Church, there are in fact twenty-three Catholic rites (Greek-Catholic rite, Ambrosian rite, etc.), each with its own liturgy, sacramental discipline, canon law and spirituality, all in full communion with the See of Rome.

As we have seen above, the Catholic Church defines herself as a communion or fellowship (*koinõnia*) that is lived out by the whole People of God together. The Church has two fundamental dimensions – an institutional-hierarchical profile (with a variety of ministries) and a charismatic dimension (with a variety of both ordinary and extraordinary charisms or 'gifts' of the Holy Spirit).

Both dimensions of the Church are co-constitutive of the Church's nature. In other words, the Church wouldn't be Church without both aspects. So, when reviewing the structures and authority of the Catholic Church, it must be born in mind that it's not simply a question of pointing to the Pope, bishops, priests and deacons. The issue is much more nuanced within the Catholic world (see www.catholicireland.net and www.catholiccommunications.url).

Through baptism, all members of the Church are called to continue Jesus' mission as Priest, Prophet and Shepherd. The authority to 'go... and make disciples of all nations' (Mt 28:19-20) is entrusted to the whole Body of Christ. Throughout the ages, members of the Church, both lay and clerical, have engaged in a wide variety of activities, prayers and ministries. Charisms of all kinds have been given to individuals and communities within the Church to carry out specific tasks and missions.

It would be difficult to assess how many religious orders, spiritual movements and currents of life have contributed to the life of the Church throughout these two millennia. And each religious order (male and female) or movement has its own structure, mode of governance and direction (see the list of orders and congregations on www.catholicireland.net). Indeed, it ought to be mentioned at this point that there is a wide variety of democratic forms within the Churches structures.

But while democratic forms are found at every level of Church life (and since Vatican II this has increased), the Church herself is not a democracy. In the Roman Catholic Church, lay and ordained ministry differ from each other 'in essence, not only in degree' (Vatican II document on the Church, *Lumen Gentium*, 10). In other words, ordained ministry is not to be understood as a 'greater' or 'higher' sharing in the baptismal priesthood common to all believers. It is something else. It 'belongs to another realm of the gifts of the Spirit' (ARCIC, *Final Report*, 13). Ultimately, God is the source of all authority in the Church. This is what the notion of a 'hierarchical' (holy origin) Church means.

Within the Catholic Church, ordained ministry serves the People of God. It is the means through which the Risen Christ, the head and spouse of the Church, continues to be present to his body and bride, the Church. Through the functions of teaching, sanctifying and community-building, the hierarchical-ordained ministry is like an objective instrument through which Christ acts. It guarantees the apostolic succession of the Church from age to age.

In other words, despite the sinfulness of a priest, a mass celebrated by him is valid. A person, who in good faith receives the Eucharist, encounters the Risen Christ and gains the benefit of that sacramental moment.

The Roman Catholic Church is made up of dioceses linked with one another in communion with the Bishop of Rome, the Pope. At every Eucharistic celebration the name of the local bishop is mentioned as well as the Pope's name. It's an expression of the points of unity and authority in the Church – the local bishop and the visible point of unity of the whole Church – the Pope.

A particularly poignant expression of a diocese's unity is the Chrism mass held on the morning of Holy Thursday each year. Representatives from all the parishes and other bodies of the diocese gather with the bishop, priests and deacons in a visible sign of the diocese's unity in communion and fellowship. Priests renew their priestly promises. They are in fact co-operators of the bishop in his mission and share in due measure in the authority that rests primarily in him.

The hierarchical structure of the Church is not simply a bureaucratic, administrative arrangement devised to respond to the question of leadership. It is the Catholic Church's belief that the evolution of the Church's essential structure is a divinely inspired evolution of the apostolic ministry described in the later books of the New Testament and witnessed to in the post-apostolic writings. Christ's own authority is shared in by various grades of ministry in various ways. Through the sacrament of Holy Orders the Church continues to be linked to the succession of faith, worship and communion that comes to us from the Apostles. It's this notion of succession that gives us the term 'Apostolic succession'.

Vatican II emphasised once more the collegial character of the episcopate and the presbyterium of priests. In other words, bishops are not isolated on their own but are members of a community of bishops and similarly for priests.

The role of the Pope is very important in Catholicism. Following the evidence in the New Testament that Peter is the head and spokesman of the twelve disciples, the Catholic Church sees in the Pope the head of the college of bishops and visible head of the Church on earth. There is a famous episode in the fifth century when it was said of Pope Leo the Great that 'Peter speaks through Leo'.

In other words, Catholics believe that the primatial role of Peter continues in a mystical manner in the Pope. The Pope is the centre and guardian of unity in the Church. From the earliest centuries we see local Churches appealing to the Bishop of Rome when there were disputes to be resolved. Vatican I defined the Pope's infallibility as an expression of the whole Church's infallibility in faith and moral teaching of divinely revealed truths. Vatican II completed this teaching when it also taught that the college of bishops, of which the Pope is head, exercises authority over the whole Church.

In recent years, there has been a discussion at an ecumenical level on how best the ministry of the Pope might be exercised in a way that would be acceptable to other Churches. The Orthodox Churches accept the role of the primacy of the Bishop of Rome was pivotal in the first millennium. The doctrine of Papal primacy is essential, but the exercise of it has a wide spectrum of possibilities.

As we have mentioned above, there is a greater stress today on structures of collaboration within the Church. It is increasing at all levels. Each diocese has an episcopal council, a council of priests, a finance committee, a college of consultors and a pastoral council, a council of Episcopal vicars for religious, associations of Christ's faithful, deaneries and parishes. Each parish in turn is encouraged to have pastoral councils, parish finance committees and work in collaboration. And, as we have mentioned each agency, religious order and movement has its own structures.

The role of women in the Church is also the subject of much comment and discussion. In Paris in 1980 Pope John Paul commented 'Just as it is true that the Church at a hierarchical level is guided by the successors of the apostles and therefore by men, it is also true that in a charismatic sense, it is women as well as men who guide it, and perhaps even more so' (See *Insegnamenti di Giovanni Paolo II*, III/1, Vatican: 1980), p. 1628). Women have recently been appointed to key positions in the Vatican.

Above all, however, we need to emphasise again that external structures are not the whole Church. In heaven, there won't be sacraments, hierarchy or charism. The three things that last from this world into heaven are – as St. Paul reminds us – faith, hope and love; 'and the greatest of these is love' (1 Cor 13:13). The Church is essentially the realm of mutual love.

Carrying on the Mission of Jesus: creating a just and inclusive society
Jesus preached the Kingdom of God. As we have seen in chapter two, this Kingdom is about a new society, one where standards and measures are different. Today one of the ways the Church continues Jesus' mission is to teach about and build up a society that is more just and inclusive. We have already looked at some of this under previous headings, especially the response in Ireland to the issue of sectarianism.

The creation of a just and inclusive society ranges from economic to political inclusion. One of the key principles in the Church's social teaching is respect for the human person (see *Catechism of the Catholic Church*, 1928-1948). As the Catechism puts it: 'Respect for the human person proceeds by way of respect for the principle that "everyone should look upon his neighbour (without any exception) as 'another self'...'". The equality of human beings is another principle. This notion of equality rests on the dignity of human beings as persons and on the rights that flow from it. There are differences that belong to God's plan and these encourage persons to practise generosity and help one another. But there are also sinful inequalities that contradict the Gospel.

A major principle in the Church's social teaching is solidarity. This is a direct demand of human and Christian fraternity. Again in the Catechism we read: 'Socio-economic problems can be resolved only with the help of all the forms of solidarity: solidarity of the poor among themselves, between rich and poor, of workers among themselves, between employers in a business, solidarity among nations and peoples. International solidarity is a requirement of the moral order; world peace depends in part upon this' (1941)

A particularly well-known agency in Ireland is the St Vincent de Paul Society (www.svp.ie), which has continued to expand and develop over the years.

The Justice Office of the Catholic Church's Conference of Religious of Ireland (CORI) has offered considerable analysis and social critique in recent years as an expression of their contribution to a more just and inclusive society (www.cori.ie/justice).

Perhaps the best-known overseas agency in Ireland is Trócaire (www.trocaire.ie). It seeks to combat issues of poverty in the most deprived areas of the world. Established in 1973, Trócaire is the official overseas development agency of the Catholic Church (see www.trocaire.org).

The word 'Trócaire' is the Irish word for 'compassion' or 'mercy'. This agency draws its inspiration from Scripture and the social teaching of the Catholic Church. It strives to promote human development and social justice in areas where the world's poorest and most oppressed people live. But it is not simply an almsgiving agency; rather, it works with and lets itself be influenced by the experiences, insights and the hopes of the poor and oppressed.

Trócaire carries out its mission through long-term development projects overseas, by providing relief during emergencies and by informing the Irish public about the root causes of poverty and injustice and mobilising the public to bring about global change.

Christian Aid is an agency similar to Trócaire although set up before it in 1945. It is the overseas agency of a number of Protestant Churches and the Anglican Communion. It funds projects in some of the world's poorest countries. It helps people to improve their own lives and to tackle the causes of poverty and injustice (www.christian-aid.org.uk).

The Corrymeela Community (www.corrymeela.org) is a community established in 1964 by Reverend Ray Davey and others. It is made up of people of all ages and Christian traditions, who, individually and together are committed to the healing of social, religious and political divisions that exist in Northern Ireland and throughout the World. It promotes an ethic of inclusion and is one of the best-known initiatives in Northern Ireland and, internationally, at this level. It has the support of members of all denominations.

The community engages in a number of projects and activities including residential twinned (Catholic/Protestant) school, youth, adult and church projects with follow-up support work. It runs open residential gatherings of members from all traditions on social, cultural, political and religious themes. It organises training and learning projects in the fields of conflict, mediation, Christian education, and so on.

Through these the community provides opportunities for meeting and dialogue so as to help dispel ignorance, prejudice and fear and to promote mutual respect, trust and co-operation between Catholics and Protestants in a spirit of reconciliation.

While the community has a centre in Ballycastle, Co. Antrim, the community itself is made up of hundreds of people dispersed around Ireland and elsewhere. The community seeks to be a sanctuary of support for victims of violence and injustice, thereby facilitating the healing of personal and social wounds. It promotes new initiatives for social and political change.

The Belfast Central Mission (www.belfastcentralmission.org) is one of the city mission agencies of the Methodist Church that seek to express Christian faith in action, through a basic respect for human dignity. It strives to commend Christian faith to others by the way the Mission responds to the needs of others. It's an example of witness teaching.

It was founded over one hundred years ago by Rev Crawford Johnson as part of the Church's response to problems typical of inner-city life such as that of Belfast. The mission meets the needs of the whole person in every dimension – spiritual, emotional, social and physical. The Belfast Central Mission continues its mission through its three congregations at Grosvenor Hall, Sandy Row and Springfield Road and through its wide range of social work projects.

SPIRASI (www.spirasi.ie) is a voluntary and intercultural humanitarian organisation run under the auspices of the congregation of the Holy Spirit. It welcomes refuge seekers including survivors of torture whatever their background, and works with them and the host community in the process of integration. To that end, Spirasi provides a variety of services including training courses, a medical programme for survivors of torture, a community awareness programme, as well as social outreach and hospitality initiatives.

Among many other projects run by religious orders, it is worth noting the Jesuit Refugee Service (www.jesuit.ie) and the Mercy Refugee Service (www.mercyworld.org), the Vincentian Refugee Centre (www.vincentians.ie).

Carrying on the mission of Jesus: a Christian vision regarding the use and sharing of the earth's resources
The last sub-section looked at some of the Christian agencies and communities involved in the sharing of the earth's resources. But increasingly, concern is expressed regarding not only the sharing but also the use of the earth's resources. The Columban missionaries, for instance, have focused on issues of ecology (www.columban.com).

The Ecumenical Patriarch of Constantinople has become a vibrant contributor to dialogue on the environmental issue, providing a faith-inspired vision for an ecological ethic that reminds the world that it is not ours to use for our own convenience. It is God's gift of love to us and we are called to return his love by protecting creation and all that is in it.

Since 1989, September 1st has been designated by the Ecumenical Patriarchate of Constantinople as a day of prayer throughout the Orthodox world for the protection of the environment.

Since that time various initiatives have been undertaken by Patriarch Bartholomew. He organised an Inter-Orthodox Conference in Crete in 1991, and has convened annual Ecological Seminars at the historic Monastery of the Holy Trinity on Halki island (near Istanbul), as a way of discerning the spiritual roots and principles of the ecological crisis. In 1995, he sponsored a symposium held on the island of Patmos on *Revelation and the Environment, AD 95 to 1995*. He also arranged a transnational conference on the Black Sea ecological crisis that included participation of all the nations that border the sea.

It is his belief that through the particular liturgical and ascetic ethos typical of Orthodox Spirituality, the Orthodox Church and leaders may provide significant moral and ethical direction toward a new generation of awareness about the planet. On June 29, 1995, both he and Pope John Paul II – who himself has also spoken out on environmental issues – signed a common declaration that included an appeal to everyone to make a determined effort to solve the current environmental problem.

In an address at the Environmental symposium at the Santa Barbara Greek Orthodox Church, California, on the 8th of November 1997, Patriarch Bartholomew described how the Eucharist is at the heart of the Church's ecological concern (www.goarch.org/patriarchate/us-visit/speeches/Address_at_ Environmenta.htm).

Inspired by the thanksgiving nature of Eucharist in which the earthly elements of bread and wine are transformed into a new creation, the Patriarch comments that 'our sin toward the world, or the spiritual root of all our pollution, lies in our refusal to view life and the world as a sacrament of thanksgiving, and as a gift of constant communion with God on a global scale'.

In expressing how every action in the world has a direct effect upon the future of the environment, he continues 'At the heart of the relationship between man and environment is the relationship between human beings. As individuals, we live not only in vertical relationships to God, and horizontal relationships to one another, but also in a complex web of relationships that extend throughout our lives, our cultures and the material world. Human beings and the environment form a seamless garment of existence; a complex fabric that we believe is fashioned by God'.

The Orthodox vision is one of the cosmos imbued with the presence of God. Our world participates, in a certain sense, in the very life of God. The famous seventh-century writer, St Maximos the Confessor, once described the world as a 'cosmic liturgy.' And it is this imagery that underlies the Patriarch's respect for the world.

The Eucharistic liturgy we celebrate is a ritual reminder of who we are and what our relationship ought to be with the cosmos: 'As human beings, created "in the image and likeness of God" (Gen 1:26), we are called to recognize this interdependence between our environment and ourselves. In the bread and the wine of the Eucharist, as priests standing before the altar of the world, we offer the creation back to the creator in relationship to Him and to each other. Indeed, in our liturgical life, we realize by anticipation, the final state of the cosmos in the Kingdom of Heaven. We celebrate the beauty of creation, and consecrate the life of the world, returning it to God with thanks. We share the world in joy as a living mystical communion with the Divine. Thus it is that we offer the fullness of creation at the Eucharist, and receive it back as a blessing, as the living presence of God'.

Care for the environment will not happen automatically. It requires asceticism, the self-control necessary to reduce our consumption in the world: 'Consuming the fruits of the earth unrestrained, we become consumed ourselves, by avarice and greed. Excessive consumption leaves us emptied, out-of-touch with our deepest self. Asceticism is a corrective practice, a vision of repentance. Such a vision will lead us from repentance to return, the return to a world in which we give, as well as take from creation'.

The Patriarch suggests we seek to help one another to understand the myriad ways in which we are related to the earth, and to one another. If we do this we may 'begin to repair the dislocation many people experience in relation to creation'. The point is that 'many human beings have come to behave as materialistic tyrants. Those that tyrannize the earth are themselves, sadly, tyrannized'.

God has called us to 'be fruitful, increase and have dominion in the earth' (Gen 1:28). But dominion is not domination. St Basil describes the creation of man in paradise on the sixth day as being the arrival of a king in his palace. It was to be lived in according to God's will and not in a way that abused the earth but rather 'to cultivate it and to guard it' (Gen 2:15).

The Patriarch draws a parallel with anti-social behaviour: 'If human beings treated one another's personal property the way they treat their environment, we would view that behaviour as anti-social. We would impose the judicial measures necessary to restore wrongly appropriated personal possessions. It is therefore appropriate, for us to seek ethical, legal recourse where possible, in matters of ecological crimes. It follows that, to commit a crime against the natural world, is a sin'.

In the light of the Patriarch's vision there are many forms of what we might call new sins: 'For humans to cause species to become extinct and to destroy the biological diversity of God's creation... for humans to degrade the integrity of earth by causing changes in its climate, by stripping the earth of its natural forests, or destroying its wetlands... for humans to injure other humans with disease... for humans to contaminate the earth's waters, its land, its air, and its life, with poisonous substances... these are sins'.

He proposes an ecological ethic. It is one that could be shared with many of the religious traditions. The issue is a priority when we consider that how we treat the earth and all of creation defines the relationship that each of us has with God. It is a barometer of how we view one another.

Carrying on the Mission of Jesus: a Christian response to dying and death
Death is the greatest mystery in life. Why death? What is there after death? What connection can we maintain with those who die? These are questions that are as much a concern today as ever.

Christianity doesn't claim the question of death is an easy one to answer! But the whole of Christian revelation – from the opening chapters of Genesis to the closing chapter of the Book of Revelation – is one great response to dying and death.

Physical death was never part of God's creative intention. It is the result of humanity's inclination to sin. The first pages of Genesis tell us, in fact, that death entered in through humanity's original turning away from God. Once separated from God, humanity lost equilibrium and became fragile to the point of death. The French theologian, Bernard Sesboüé writes: 'The death which we experience is the result of a disorder introduced into our relationship with the world and with nature by human sin, that is to say, by the initial rejection of God's gift' (*The Resurrection and the Life*, Collegeville: Liturgical Press, 1996, p. 59). Eternal life, however, is offered to us in Jesus Christ, our Saviour. The Christian belief is that this eternal life begins in baptism but that our whole life is a journey to the fullness of this eternal life in heaven. Death, then, is the road that takes us from the world to another realm. 'But this is no safe passage, for those who have the misfortune to undertake such a journey in the state of sin, eternal death will be their destiny; but for those who journey in the company of Christ's salvation, eternal life in God will be their destiny' (Sesboüé, p. 60).

Christian doctrine maintains that death is the separation of body and soul. The soul should be understood not as a part of the human body alongside the physical aspect, but rather in the biblical sense as the vital principle of a human being, the 'me', the centre of the person that remains after death.

Christians see death not as something to be passively endured, but as an act to accomplish. The great gift God has given us is freedom. It is up to us whether we choose to live in such a way as to enter eternal life or to build our life on the vanity that passes away with death.

Catholics believe that God also gives Purgatory to those who die desiring heaven but not yet ready to enter into its perfection of love. It is true that the imagery associated with the notion of Purgatory and Hell does not speak to many today. Much of the imagery itself is the product of literary imagination. Today there is a return to what revelation teaches us about these realities. What we see is that revelation is quite sober in its language. It doesn't intend to give graphic descriptions of Purgatory or Hell.

Purgatory is to be understood not so much as a punishment but rather as a gift of healing and transformation to achieve our full conversion to love before entering heaven. 'As the father met the prodigal son, so God meets us with open arms and then clothes us with the best robe. He cannot allow his children to enter the family home dirty and dressed in rags. To enter the banquet of the king, one must be clothed in the wedding garment' (Sesboüé, p. 91). In other words, if at death, we are not yet fully clothed for heaven, but genuinely desire it, God gives us an opportunity to prepare.

It is Christian belief that because of the death and resurrection of Jesus Christ, all human beings are offered the opportunity to die in Christ and so rise with him. As the Vatican II document on the Church in the modern world puts it: 'For since Christ died for everyone... we must hold that the Holy Spirit offers to all the possibility of being made partners, in a way known to God, in the paschal mystery' (*Gaudium et Spes*, 22).

Because the divine-human Son of God, Jesus Christ, has entered into our human condition right to the point of death, our life, suffering and death can be united to his in a way that makes us share in his death and resurrection (Rom 6:2-11; 2 Cor 4:10-12). This is, in fact, what happens in baptism – we enter into the mystery of his death and resurrection. And death is the ultimate 'ratification of our baptism, the fullness of our death to sin and entry into the resurrection of Christ' (Sesboüé, p. 62).

Christians see natural death, therefore, as a gift of themselves to God. Already, throughout their lives, they prepare for the hour of their death by dying to themselves in love of God and their neighbour. All suffering and death is a way for Christians to 'complete what is lacking in Christ's afflictions for the sake of his body, that is, the Church' (Col 1:24). Dying and death, lived as a gift of ourselves to God and as a sharing in Christ's suffering and death, can be a final act of love before we meet the God who is love, face to face.

The Church accompanies those who are dying with great care. She offers three sacraments to assist them: the sacrament of reconciliation actualises the grace of baptism; the anointing of the sick is a new confirmation, a gift of the strength of the Holy Spirit in times of illness and crisis; and the Eucharist, the viaticum, the 'food of immortality' as Ignatius of Antioch, one of the early martyrs of the Church, called it, is our final food for the journey from this life to the next.

Many Christian religious orders, associations and lay men and women dedicate their lives in discipleship of Jesus Christ by attending in particular to the care of the dying. The well-known contemporary order of the Missionaries of Charity, established by Saint Mother Teresa, is a case in point. It became famous for the sisters' care of the destitute, abandoned and dying of all castes and religions in Calcutta.

Mother Teresa began simply going out to the poorest of poor, especially those dying on the streets of Calcutta. Soon others joined her. They began to bring the dying home to their premises and look after them. The motivating spark for this action was their radical desire to see Jesus, especially in the poor and in those dying and abandoned. When they would bring the dying home, they bathed their wounds and helped them to die with dignity, in peace and surrounded by the love of Jesus.

For Mother Teresa, it was a question of surrounding the person with love as he or she approached that definitive encounter with Jesus in death. She wrote: 'The dying, the cripple, the mental, the unwanted, the unloved – they are Jesus in disguise' and 'It is not how much we do, but how much love we put in the doing. It is not how much we give, but how much love we put in the giving'.

It is this love that best responds to the dying persons' deepest needs. It is this love that motivates countless initiatives of Christians throughout the world to accompany those who are dying in the solemn journey into the Resurrection and the Life.

Two contemporary understandings of Jesus

Jürgen Moltmann

Jürgen Moltmann is one of the most influential of contemporary German Protestant theologians. As a young man he experienced the horror of World War II. He also became a prisoner of war. The gruesome depth of inhumanity reached during the War caused him to ask: how can we speak of God and how can we do theology after Auschwitz? It was this experience of war and his recognition of the oppression, injustice and poverty in the world that made Moltmann interested in the social and political implications of Christianity.

The influences on his theology include the theologians Dietrich Bonhoeffer and Karl Barth, the Scripture scholars, Ernst Käsemann and Gerhard von Rad, and the Jewish Marxist philosopher Ernst Bloch. His theology became a major influence on liberation theologies.

A major focus in Moltmann's theology is eschatology. In other words, the need to focus again on the futuristic expectations – just like the early Christian community. They looked to the future, believing in the resurrection of Jesus from the dead, Jesus' promise of the coming of the Spirit and the second coming.

In his work, *The Theology of Hope*, Moltmann contends that 'from first to last, and not merely in the epilogue, Christianity is eschatology, is hope' (London: SCM 1967, p. 16). It is hope in the radically new future of the eschatological kingdom that makes us see this world with new eyes.

God's promise is that this world subject to sin and suffering will be transformed in God's new creation. Because of Jesus' resurrection from the dead, that transformation is already underway. While history is moving towards the second coming of Jesus, it is being drawn like a magnet towards him because he is already coming towards us from the future.

Hope in the resurrection prompts us to engage with possibilities for change in this world, not allowing things to stand still and to work for a better world. The eschatological dimension of our faith serves as a critique of this world's unjust structures.

Another key concern for Moltmann is the importance for Christians to have a Christianised understanding of God! His book, *The Trinity and the Kingdom of God* (London: SCM, 1980) outlines his (and this is shared also by other theologians) fear that the notion of God which many Christians have is not really Christian in the sense that it is a vague, philosophical or generalised notion of a monarchical God figure. But God is Trinity. Moltmann invites us to view all our understanding of creation, reconciliation and glorification as revolving around our sharing in the mutual love between God the Father, Son and Holy Spirit, a life of divine mutual love that has been revealed to us in Jesus Christ.

The Christian notion of God must always start, therefore, from Jesus Christ. Moltmann has dedicated a number of books to Christology: *The Crucified God* (1973), 'possibly the most important theological book to be published in the second half of the twentieth century' (Macquarrie, *Jesus Christ in Modern Thought*, London: SCM, 1990, p. 321); *The Way of Jesus Christ* (London: SCM, 1981) and *Jesus Christ for Today's World* (London: SCM, 1994). This last work is short and very readable, a useful summary of many of his Christological concerns.

What Moltmann underlines is that it is in the light of the crucified Jesus Christ that we see the revelation of God. Here we see God participating in our human suffering. In his theology he echoes the Reformed tradition of emphasising Jesus' cry of abandonment on the cross: 'my God, my God, why have you forsaken me?' (Mk 15: 34). This, for Moltmann, has to be the centre of Christian thinking. Not without controversy, he writes of a God who suffers, involved in our suffering, because he is love.

Normally, it is said that God, precisely because he is God, cannot suffer and this is the very reason he is always present to us as the stable ground of our being. In other words, we may waver, but God is always there in strength, constant love and fidelity. Jesus, it is said, suffers in his humanity not in his divinity. But Moltmann wants to reclaim the biblical vision of God as involved in our history and therefore also in some way in suffering.

In writing about the event of the cross, Moltmann stresses the closeness of God the Father and Jesus. He also seems to indicate, however, that, not only did Jesus feel himself abandoned by God the Father, but he really was abandoned. If that were the case, it would be a statement too far. However, it is clear that Moltmann wants to emphasise the total empathy of Jesus with suffering humanity. He writes: 'The history of Christ with God and of God with Christ becomes the history of God with us and hence our history with God' (*The Crucified God*, p. 277).

The aspects of death, suffering and the poverty of our human history have been taken up into the history of God. Moltmann cites a famous episode from a passage in Elie Wiesel's novel, *Night*, describing an execution at Auschwitz. As the crowd watches three people die by hanging, someone asked: 'where is God?'. Moltmann wants to answer by saying that God is there in that execution.

Through the cross of Christ, God knows our suffering and death. He knows what death is like from within, as it were. And he knows not just individual death, but also the death-scenarios facing humanity today. Jesus suffered vicariously the end-time sufferings that threaten the whole creation. In the event of the Cross Jesus was undergoing the birth-pangs of the new creation. His resurrection is the eschatological new creation of all of nature.

In his book, *The Way of Jesus Christ*, these themes are all developed further. He continues to read Jesus' resurrection as opening up an eschatological future for us that is always greater than we can imagine. The resurrection of Jesus is real and not simply a mythology. Jesus' resurrection is the end of the kind of history we are used to talking about in positivistic terms (facts, figures, dates) and opens up a new history, the history of the new realm, the new creation that has already begun to develop within this world, but will ultimately blossom in the next with the coming of Jesus Christ at the parousia.

For Moltmann, Jesus Christ is 'on his way' to the messianic future, so our understanding of Jesus has to be something dynamic not static. In investigating the earthly life and ministry of Jesus, Moltmann emphasises how his life and mission were always directed to the Father and the Spirit. He draws our attention especially to the action and power of the Spirit both in Jesus' life and now in the time of the Church.

For Moltmann Christology is inseparable from 'christopraxis'. Who we say Jesus is and how we live go together. It is in living and following Jesus' way of life in a community of discipleship that we know and understand him. For Moltmann holistic Christology, soteriology (the doctrine of our salvation) and ethics are all linked. And the Kingdom of God is a central notion linking all of this: 'if we want to understand who Jesus really is, we have to experience the Kingdom of God' (*Jesus Christ for Today's world*, p. 7). It is a Kingdom that involves liberation at all levels of human existence.

In more recent years Moltmann has developed his thought on a 'cosmic' Christology. Drawing upon theologians such as Teilhard de Chardin and Karl Rahner, he reflects on Christ as the Logos, the Word through whom the worlds were created and he sees implications in this for environmental issues.

Chiara Lubich
Chiara Lubich, the founder of the Focolare Movement, is one of the best-known spiritual writers today. On the basis of her Christian experience and spirituality her writings can be considered also under the heading of Christology.

Like Moltmann, she experienced the horror and the destruction of life and relationship during World War II. She herself had to suspend her philosophy studies because of the war. But, together with her companions, she discovered the Gospel in a way that was to change their lives (for a biographical introduction see Jim Gallagher, *Chiara Lubich: A Woman's Work*, London: HarperCollins, 1997).

Initially influenced by the Franciscan spirituality, during the war she and her companions realised that the Gospel was not just a book of consolation but also words to be put into practice concretely. Its words were universal, suitable for every place and every situation in life.

The Gospel brought them to see the various faces of Jesus that surrounded them everyday. It was an experience of the closeness of God who is Love. In the light of sentences such as 'as you did it to one of the least of these my brethren, you did it to me' (Mt 25:40), they realised that Jesus was present in the poor, in those orphaned because of war, in each other as brothers and sisters, and in every neighbour who is a presence of Jesus. He was also to be found in the Eucharist and in the bishop (Lk 10:16)

Gradually they began to perceive a new light, ardour, joy and peace within them, and they realised that this was the result of a particular presence of Jesus among them, because they were trying to remain united in his name as the Gospel says: 'For where two or three are gathered in my name, there am I in the midst of them' (Mt 18:20).

They had come to understand that to gather in the name of Jesus meant living together Jesus' New Commandment (Jn 13:34) with the measure of his self-giving. It meant not simply going to God on their own, in an individual relationship with God, but rather going to God together in a lived communion based on the Word, the Eucharist and mutual love. And this was what brought a new joy into their lives. Soon, in fact, many others were joining with them in living this new experience of the Gospel.

Writing some years later of what she and the other members of this new community discovered at this time, Chiara Lubich commented: 'Where there were two or more from different countries, the barrier of nationalism crumbled. Where there were two or more from different racial backgrounds, racism crumbled. Two or more – whoever they were, even when they had always been considered incompatible for reasons of culture, class, age, or whatever... All could be, and indeed were meant to be, united in the name of Christ' (quoted in Judith M. Povilis, *United in his Name*, New York: New City, 1992, p. 102).

It seemed to them they were sharing already, in some way, what we will experience fully in heaven: our insertion in Jesus Christ into the dynamic and constantly new life of the Trinity, the life of mutual love between the Father, Son and Holy Spirit.

They understood more of what was coming to life among them when they were reading the Gospel one day in the air-raid shelter by candlelight. They opened John's Gospel, chapter 17, and read: 'May they all be one... so that the world may believe...' (Jn 17:21). They asked Jesus to teach them how to be builders of unity.

A very important moment for them was one day when a priest told them his opinion as to when Jesus had suffered the most. At that time people traditionally said it was in the garden of Gethsemane that he suffered the moment. But the priest commented that he believed that it was when he cried out on the Cross: 'My God, my God, why have you forsaken me?' (Mt 27:46; Mk 15:34).

This became a turning point for the new movement of young men and women that was coming to life. They realised that, if this was the moment Jesus suffered the most, it was also the moment he loved the most; because the cry of Jesus on the Cross includes all our 'whys'.

It was through his cry on the Cross that Jesus took on and transformed all our divisions and darkness and introduced us into the unity he has in his relationship with the Father and the Spirit. They realised they could recognise and love Jesus Crucified and Forsaken in any darkness, poverty and division within themselves and in the life of their neighbours. By loving him that way they could become builders of unity.

Chiara Lubich's spirituality has resulted in new perspectives for theology, also in the area of Christology (e.g., Piero Coda *et* al., *An Introduction to the Abba School*, New York: New City, 2002, and Marisa Cherini, *God who is love in the experience and thought of Chiara Lubich*, New York: New City, 1992). As M.D. Chenu has shown, throughout the ages spiritualities have expressed themselves in theology. In recent years there is a growing appreciation of the link between theology and spirituality. M. Schneider has pointed out that 'a Church which is founded on the "apostles and prophets" (Eph 2:20), on ministry and charism... cannot but remain fruitfully enriched by the interdependence of theology and sanctity, theological doctrine and "theology lived"'.

The Christology in Chiara Lubich's writings such as *The Cry* (New York: New City, 2001), *Secret of Unity* (London: New City, 1985) and *Jesus in the Midst* (New York: New City, 1976) revolves around two centres: Jesus' prayer for unity in John's Gospel 'May they all be one' (Jn 17:21), and Jesus' cry on the Cross: 'My God, my God, why have you forsaken me?' (Mk 15:34; Mt 27:46). Lubich reads Jesus' life and ministry from this two-in-one perspective of the Trinitarian unity Jesus brought on earth and the love that has its measure in Jesus' laying down his life.

She emphasises the eschatological dimension of the Kingdom of God that Jesus proclaimed and spread. It is a reality 'already' present among us when we love one another, but it will be 'even more' an experience of love and unity in the heart of God the Father (*Abbà*) in heaven. Our actions and projects in life will be transfigured in the new heavens and the new earth that we are called already by Jesus Christ to build up in love. 'It is not the "what" we do but the "how" that matters'.

Similar to Moltmann, therefore, Lubich sees Christopraxis and Christology as inseparable. We know Christ only when we live his art of loving contained in the Gospel. Knowledge of Jesus Christ is an experience lived more than a mental exercise to be worked out. But, in entering into the Gospel as a way of life, we discover the wisdom of Jesus Christ that also informs mind and will, heart and concrete action.

Arising from her Christology, Lubich highlights the communitarian aspect of Christian living. For her what is distinctive of Christianity is that we go to God together and not on our own.

She takes seriously the humanity of Jesus. Christianity can never simply be limited to the religious or spiritual realm. It must also impact on the social and concrete dimensions of human existence. Jesus is the God-*Man*: 'To separate him from the total life of a person is a practical heresy of our times'.

Accordingly, in latter years Lubich has launched an interdisciplinary study centre and a number of projects in various fields such as economics and politics, art and psychology, sport and media, as well as theology and philosophy (www.focolare.org and www. edc-online.org/defaultE.htm).

Conclusion: Mary, the first disciple

This book on Christianity's origins and contemporary expression would be incomplete without a final reference to the woman who has often been called Jesus' 'first disciple': Mary. The place of Mary has long been prominent in the Roman Catholic and Orthodox Traditions of the Church, and it is not absent in other traditions. In fact, one of the recent developments in ecumenical dialogue has been a new interest in Mary.

The few but very significantly placed references to Mary in the Gospel indicate her importance for the early Christian community. Throughout the centuries, Christians have gained deeper insights – through their contemplation and living out of Scripture – into this woman most written about in Western literature and depicted in Western art.

The Council of Ephesus spoke of her as the 'Mother of God' (*Theotokos*, god-bearer). Based on Scriptural motifs, authors have written of her as daughter of God the Father, as well as the 'New Eve', co-operator with (and in this sense bride of) Christ (see Jn 2: 1-11; 1 Cor 3:9; Eph 2 and 5). Her close link with the Holy Spirit (Lk 1:35) has also been emphasised.

As the woman who accompanied Jesus from his conception right through childhood, his public ministry and then to his death on the cross, Mary is the best person to teach us who Jesus is and how to follow him. Her spiritual journey as a 'disciple' of Jesus is like a model for all Christians and for the whole Church.

Mary is important as we go about interpreting the Christian message for today. And not just Mary as an individual but all that she stands for in the Church: the existential 'yes' to God, holiness, prophecy, saints and mystics, laity, women, charisms and new ecclesial movements, outreach, social projects and concrete service in bringing the presence of Christ into the world. The Church, after all, is not just an organisation that gets things done. It's not just the hierarchical structures that mediate Christ through sacramental grace. The Church is, above all, a way of life that Jesus brought on earth. And Mary was the first to live this new way of life.

It has been said that without attention to this Marian aspect, 'Christianity threatens imperceptibly to become inhuman. The Church becomes functionalistic, soulless, a hectic enterprise without any point of rest, estranged from its true nature by the planners. And because, in this manly-masculine world, all that we have is one ideology replacing another, everything becomes polemical, critical, bitter, humourless, and ultimately boring, and people in their masses run away from such a Church...' (Hans Urs von Balthasar, *Elucidations*, San Francisco: Ignatius Press, 1998, pp. 112-113).

The point being made here is that the Church is made up of many dimensions and profiles. During his life on earth Jesus was surrounded by various persons such as Mary his mother, his cousin, John the Baptist, his friends, Martha and Mary, the disciples, the twelve apostles and so on. Through the Holy Spirit, their faith experiences flow into the Church as constitutive profiles or missions that now continue in the life of the Church.

We are used to seeing the 'Petrine' profile reflected in the Pope, bishops and priests, but the Church is multi-layered. We need to recognised that there are also other profiles of the Church such as the dimension of John the Baptist that continues in martyrdom, the profile of Martha and Mary that continues also in the aspect of care and hospitality, the Pauline level of novelty and charism that is seen in new forms of life in the Church, the continuing profile of tradition associated with the apostle James as well as the continuing profile of prayer and mysticism linked, for instance, with John, the beloved disciple.

There are many dimensions of the Church and, as Pope John Paul has commented, the Marian profile is in many ways the deepest aspect of the Church, the one that summarises and embraces all others. Without her 'yes' (Mary was a lay woman who knew how to love and to suffer) we would have none of the rest. It is the Marian aspect that is emerging more clearly at this time of the Church's journey.

Christianity is now into the third millennium of its history. In many ways, however, it is only beginning! It's a time when Christians are being invited to 'start again' from scratch, from a rediscovery of the novelty of the Gospel of Jesus Christ. And Mary has been called the 'star' of this New Evangelisation.